HOTSPOTS
HAWA

June 25th 20

To Debo + Liam,

Happy Honeymoon

Love
Megg xx

Written by Pam Mandel

Published by Thomas Cook Publishing
A division of Thomas Cook Tour Operations Limited
Company registration no. 1450464 England
The Thomas Cook Business Park, Unit 9, Coningsby Road,
Peterborough PE3 8SB, United Kingdom
Email: books@thomascook.com, Tel: + 44 (0) 1733 416477
www.thomascookpublishing.com

Produced by Cambridge Publishing Management Limited
Burr Elm Court, Main Street, Caldecote CB23 7NU

ISBN: 978-1-84157-979-5

First edition © 2008 Thomas Cook Publishing
Text © Thomas Cook Publishing,
Maps © Thomas Cook Publishing/PCGraphics (UK) Limited

Project Editor: Karen Fitzpatrick
Production/DTP: Steven Collins

Printed and bound in Spain by GraphyCems

Cover photography © 4-CR/Giovanni Simeone

CONTENTS

WHAT'S IN YOUR GUIDEBOOK?

Independent authors Impartial, up-to-date information from our travel experts who meticulously source local knowledge.

Experience Thomas Cook's 165 years in the travel industry and guidebook publishing enriches every word with expertise you can trust.

Travel know-how Contributions by thousands of staff around the globe, each one living and breathing travel.

Editors Travel-publishing professionals, pulling everything together to craft a perfect blend of words, pictures, maps and design.

You, the traveller We deliver a practical, no-nonsense approach to information, geared to how you really use it.

ABOUT THE AUTHOR

Freelance writer and photographer Pam Mandel lives in Seattle, Washington. She never leaves home without a passport, a camera, and a ukulele. She keeps a blog about her adventures at
Ⓦ www.nerdseyeview.com

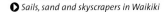 *Sails, sand and skyscrapers in Waikiki*

INTRODUCTION
Getting to know Hawaii

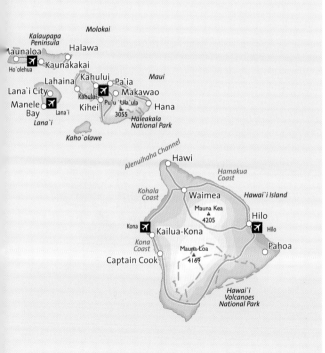

Getting to know Hawaii

A legend tells of how mythical Maui used his magic hook to pull the Hawaiian Islands out of the sea. During this epic fishing expedition, Maui told his brothers to paddle fiercely and keep their eyes forward. One brother looked back, the line snapped, the magic hook was lost – and only those islands that had already broken the surface of the ocean remain.

Geology explains in a rather different way how these islands appeared in the middle of the Pacific Ocean, approximately 3,800 km (2,361 miles) from the United States mainland. The islands are the exposed peaks of volcanoes rising from the Pacific floor. Mauna Loa and Kilauea are still active – others are dormant.

While all the islands have their own unique characteristics, they share the effects of the tropical climate and offer a startling variety of ecosystems. The larger islands have a dry side and a wet side: low scrub, lava floes, drier days are set against tropical growth, steep cliffs and waterfalls, more rain – and more rainbows.

⬥ *A traditional tiki wood carving at Kona Resort*

The temperate waters are home to brightly coloured tropical fish. Dolphins play here; humpback whales pass through every season on their migrations. The climate encourages the growth of coffee, pineapple and sugar, and newer additions like vanilla and lavender.

The earliest occupancy of Hawaii dates back to AD 300–750, when Polynesians arrived from Tahiti via outrigger canoe. Hawaii's exposure to the West began with the arrival of British explorer Captain James Cook, who met an untimely end when relations with the natives went sour. Unified under King Kamehameha the Great in 1810, the Kingdom of Hawaii was an independent nation until Queen Lili`uokalani was forced to abdicate her throne in 1894. Hawaii became a US state in 1959.

Native Hawaiian culture suffered years of assault by missionaries and opportunists. The graceful *hula*, Hawaii's traditional dance, was outlawed, and the modest all-covering muumuu introduced. Hawaiian culture has also been changed by the influx of immigrants from around the world. The Portuguese arrived with the ukulele, an instrument now synonymous with Hawaiian music. Plantation labourers from Japan, China, the Philippines and other Pacific-facing nations brought their own additions to a changing land. Now, native Hawaiian culture is in resurgence, with Hawaiian music, *hula* and language earning the interest of locals and visitors alike.

HAWAIIAN PLACE NAMES

Although the 'okina' mark (or glottal stop) is accurately found in the names of every island except Maui – that is, O`ahu, Kaua`i, Hawai`i, Moloka`i, Lana`i, Ni`ihau and Kaho`olawe – you'll rarely see them used in conventional English spellings, and the official name of the US state is simply 'Hawaii'.

This book uses okinas in the following cases: for the island of Hawai`i (usually called the Big Island), to distinguish it from Hawaii the state or former kingdom; for place and proper names on the islands themselves; and for the islands of Ni`ihau and Kaho`olawe, since they are still considered sites of traditional and cultural importance to native Hawaiians.

THE BEST OF HAWAII

Swaying palm trees, surf, golden sand...the tropical escape of Hawaii
is much as travellers imagine it to be. But the islands offer more,
with a landscape that goes from high peaks to deep canyons.
So while tourism continues to boom, and glittering new hotels,
resorts and shopping centres line the promenades, it's still possible
to get away from it all.

TOP 10 ATTRACTIONS

- **Hot lava, steaming vents, live volcanoes** Yellow sulphur, cracks in
  the earth's crust, and, when it's flowing, red hot lava, the active
  volcanoes of Mauna Loa, Mauna Kea and Haleakala (on Maui
  and the Big Island) are a geological wonderland (see pages 42, 51
  and 82).

- **The City of Refuge on the Big Island** Where refugees once sought
  absolution, wooden warriors guard the shores while sea turtles
  bask on the protected sands (see page 41).

- **The Road to Hana on Maui** Wayside parks, pools, streams, views
  and more than 600 curves on a 95-km (60-mile) scenic drive that
  ends near cascading pools at `Ohe`o Gulch (see page 80).

- **Kauai's Na Pali Coast** Experience the place where green cathedral
  cliffs plunge into the turquoise ocean – from the air, the deck of a
  boat or on foot (see page 62).

- **Sand and surf on Oahu's North Shore** Golden beaches and surf make the North Shore world-famous for surfing (see page 29).

- **Abundant sea life** The waters around the islands are home to majestic humpback whales, dolphins, sea turtles and tropical fish, making snorkelling a must (see page 41).

- **Hawaiian music and dance** Experience live *aloha* with the beauty of *hula* and the sounds of steel and ukulele (see page 108).

- **The glitter and glam of Waikiki** High-end fashion, gourmet restaurants, live music in the bars and on the beach – street life and beach life where the waves meet the shore (see page 20).

- **Time travel to old Hawaii in Molokai's Halawa Valley** You'll need a guide for a visit to this private place of taro patches, storytellers and sacred waterfalls (see page 87).

- **The feast and festivity of a *lu`au*** The heart-stopping sound of the drums, the swaying hips of the Tahitian dancers, the thrill of fire dancers and the food, the food, the food (see page 96).

❖ *The beautiful tropical coastline at Makena*

SYMBOLS KEY

The following symbols are used throughout this book:

ⓐ address ☎ telephone ⓦ website address
🕒 opening times ❶ important

The following symbols are used on the maps:

✉	post office	⭕	city
🛍	shopping	⚪	small town
✈	airport	▨	POI (point of interest)
➕	hospital	═	motorway
🛡	police station	—	main road
✝	church		minor road
		—	railway

❶ numbers denote featured cafés, restaurants & evening venues

RESTAURANT CATEGORIES
The symbol after the name of each restaurant listed in this guide
indicates the price of a typical main course plus starter or dessert
and drink for one person.
£ under US$15   ££ US$16–30   £££ more than US$30

▶ *Ready for surfing!*

RESORTS
The islands & excursions

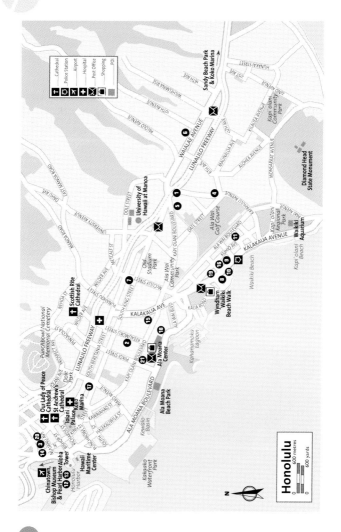

Honolulu

Honolulu

Hawaii's capital city, Honolulu, sits on a crescent of golden sand on the southern shores of Oahu Island. Beach boys and girls play in the waves, sailing boats slide across the water, and holidaymakers walk along streets lined with glittering shops and high-rise hotels. Tourists from around the world flock to Hawaii's hub, learning to surf by day and dining and dancing after the sun goes down.

Game fishing, snorkelling and sightseeing tour boats leave from Honolulu Harbor; buses unload groups of tourists at the historic landmark of Pearl Harbor. Honolulu may well be Hawaii's liveliest city – certainly it offers the most shopping and nightlife of anywhere on the islands.

But in spite of the crowds, the city beaches are surprisingly appealing – and are perhaps at their best at sundown, viewed from the beachside bar of some iconic hotel, a Mai Tai in hand, while the sun sets over Waikiki Beach. Travellers seeking that perfect concoction of urban beach life will love Waikiki.

BEACHES

Ala Moana Beach Park

Near the Ala Moana Shopping Center, this beach provides good swimming for kids. There are lifeguards, public toilets, showers and picnic areas. It's popular with locals.

Kapi`olani Park & Queen's Beach

An easy walk from the centre of Waikiki, there is good snorkelling and swimming to be enjoyed here.

Sandy Beach Park

On the southern tip of Oahu: big waves for body boarders and big winds for kites. The beach has public toilets, showers, picnic areas, free parking and lifeguards. Ask about swimming conditions before venturing in, since the surf can be high and dangerous.

Waikiki Beach

Waikiki Beach lies at the centre of the Waikiki scene, which caters for surfing, swimming and snorkelling, and is walking distance from almost all Waikiki hotels. Gear rental and surfing lessons are available on the beach.

THINGS TO SEE & DO

Bishop Museum

Hawaii's largest museum was founded by Charles Reed Bishop to house the collection of Hawaiian artefacts and family heirlooms of Princess Bernice Pauahi Bishop, the last descendant of the royal Kamehameha family. In addition to the cultural artefacts, the museum also has natural history and science exhibits and a planetarium.

ⓐ 1525 Bernice St, Honolulu ⓘ 847 3511 ⓦ www.bishopmuseum.org
ⓛ 09.00–17.00 daily ⓘ Admission charge

🔺 *Bishop Museum has striking cultural and natural history collections*

🔺 Aloha *wear and ukuleles are favourites with tourists*

Chinatown

Adventurous eaters and shoppers will find edibles and otherwise from China, Vietnam, the Philippines, Korea, Hawaii and many other cultures in this lively neighbourhood. Chinatown is also home to galleries and nightlife, going from ethnic diversity by day to artsy and hip by night.
🅐 Centred on Hotel St between River & Bethel Sts

`Iolani Palace

This royal palace was home to Hawaii's last reigning monarchs, King Kalakaua and his sister, Queen Lili`uokalani, who ruled following Kalakaua's death. The queen was held captive in her own home as the monarchy was overthrown. Today, the restored palace hosts exhibitions and events, including free concerts by the Royal Hawaiian Band.
🅐 Corner of King & Richards Sts 🅣 538 1471 🅦 www.iolanipalace.org
🅛 09.00–16.30 (self-guided tour); 09.00–11.15 (guided tour) Tues–Sat
🅘 Admission charge
Ticket office 🅘 522 0832 🅛 08.00–16.00 Mon–Sat

Pearl Harbor

When the Empire of Japan bombed Pearl Harbor on 7 December 1941, the United States entered World War II. This historic harbour is home to a number of military memorials and attractions, the most popular being the USS *Arizona* Memorial.

USS *Arizona* Memorial The memorial marks the last resting place of many of the 1,177 servicemen who died in the attack on Pearl Harbor. The memorial spans the centre of the sunken battleship. A visitor's centre provides historical context and background. Allow plenty of time to visit the memorial – two hours is considered a typical waiting time in the visitor's centre. Security is strict and you might be required to leave your bag or rucksack in storage during your visit. ⓐ 1 Arizona Memorial Place ⓣ 422 2771 ⓦ www.nps.gov/usar ⓛ 07.30–17.00 daily ⓘ Admission free

⬥ *Visit the historic site of Pearl Harbor*

USS *Bowfin* Submarine Museum and Park Explore naval history and then visit a once-operative submarine. The crew on the submarine tell stories and answer questions about life on a working submarine. ⓐ 1 Arizona Memorial Place ⓣ 836 0317 ⓦ www.bowfin.org ⓛ 08.00–17.00 daily ❶ Admission charge

Battleship *Missouri* Memorial This refurbished battleship – nicknamed the Mighty Mo – was the site of the Japanese Empire's surrender to the Allied forces. Built in 1944, the ship remained in commission until 1992. ⓐ 1 Arizona Memorial Place ⓣ 423 2263 ⓦ www.ussmissouri.org ⓛ 09.00–17.00 daily ❶ Admission charge

Waikiki Aquarium Learn about the creatures that inhabit the tropical Pacific and the waters surrounding the Hawaiian Islands at the aquarium in Kapi`olani Park, which is walking distance from most Waikiki hotels. ⓐ 2777 Kalakaua Ave ⓣ 923 9741 ⓦ www.waquarium.org ⓛ 09.00–16.30 daily ❶ Admission charge

TAKING A BREAK

Leonard's Bakery £ ❶ *Malasadas* – a sweet fried doughnut – are made fresh here, while you wait. ⓐ 933 Kapahulu Ave ⓣ 737 5591 ⓦ www.leonardshawaii.com ⓛ 06.00–21.00 daily

Like Like Drive-In £ ❷ Diner-style local food including eggs and rice and *saimin* (egg noodles in soup). ⓐ 745 Keeaumoku St ⓣ 941 2515 ⓛ 24 hours daily

Grand Café and Bakery ££ ❸ Fresh food and pastries in an original Chinatown bakery just off Nuuanu Ave. ⓐ 31 North Pauahi St ⓣ 531 0001 ⓦ www.grandcafeandbakery.com ⓛ 07.00–13.30 Tues, 07.00–13.30 & 17.15–20.00 Wed–Fri, 08.00–13.00 & 17.15–20.00 Sat, 08.00–13.00 Sun

● *City meets sea at Waikiki Bay*

AFTER DARK

A night out in Waikiki is incomplete without a walk down 'the strip',
Kalakaua Avenue. You'll find musicians playing 'Jawaiian' (a combination
of Jamaican reggae and Hawaiian music), magicians performing
sleight-of-hand feats, spray-paint artists and an endless parade of
visitors and locals checking each other out.

Restaurants
Ono Hawaiian Foods £ ❹ This casual place serves up big plates of local
food. '*Ono*' means delicious in Hawaiian. ❷ 726 Kapahulu Ave ❸ 737 2275
🕐 11.00–20.00 Mon–Sat

Izakaya Nonbei ££ ❺ The menu can be difficult to navigate for first timers, so put yourself in the hands of the staff and don't be afraid to ask questions. Casual Japanese dining off Kapi`olani Boulevard. ⓐ 3108 Olu St ⓣ 734 5573 ⓛ 17.00–23.30 daily

Town ££ ❻ Local and (when possible) organic ingredients, Mediterranean-inspired bistro food and signature cocktails. ⓐ 3435 Waialae Ave, Suite 103 ⓣ 735 5900 ⓦ www.townkaimuki.com ⓛ 06.30–21.30 Mon–Sat

Chef Mavro's £££ ❼ Superior French-inspired cuisine made from fresh Hawaiian ingredients. Set menus and plates paired with wines. ⓐ 1969 South King St ⓣ 944 4714 ⓦ www.chefmavro.com ⓛ Tues–Sun evening only ❶ Reservations required

Nobu £££ ❽ Exotic Japanese cuisine at the Waikiki Parc Hotel off Kalakaua Avenue. ⓐ 2233 Helumoa Rd ⓣ 237 6999 ⓦ www.noburestaurants.com ⓛ 11.30–14.00 & 17.30–23.00 Mon–Fri, 17.30–23.00 Sat & Sun ❶ Reservations required, phone lines open from 10.00

Bars

The Banyan Court ££ ❾ Watch the sun set to the sounds of Hawaiian music at the Moana Surfrider Hotel. ⓐ 2365 Kalakaua Ave ⓣ 922 3111 ⓦ www.moana-surfrider.com ⓛ 10.30–24.00 daily

Mai Tai Bar ££ ❿ Views of the beach accompany Mai Tai cocktails at the famous pink Royal Hawaiian Hotel. The hotel will be closing for renovation for several months from June 2008. ⓐ 2259 Kalakaua Ave ⓣ 923 7311 ⓦ www.royal-hawaiian.com ⓛ 10.30–00.30 daily

The Yard House ££ ⓫ A lively sports bar with 130 beers on tap and full restaurant just off Ala Wai Boulevard. ⓐ 220 Kapuni St ⓣ 923 9274 ⓦ www.yardhouse.com ⓛ 11.00–01.00 or later daily

Sunset cruises

Look back at the glittering skyline of Waikiki while you cruise and have drinks, dinner and even enjoy live music. Some tours provide transportation to and from your hotel. Reservations are required.

Ali'i Kai ££ ⑫ This affordable two-hour informal buffet cruise includes live music and dancing. Departs daily from Pier 5 at Aloha Tower. Kids are welcome on board. Book through Roberts Hawaii. ⓐ Pier 5 at Aloha Tower ⓣ 954 8652 ⓛ Daily

Star of Honolulu ££–£££ ⑬ Pick your package on this 500-passenger dinner cruise ship. Departs from Pier 8 at Aloha Tower. ⓐ Pier 8 at Aloha Tower ⓣ 983 STAR (7827) ⓦ www.starofhonolulu.com ⓛ Daily

Live music

Pick up *Honolulu Weekly* for the entertainment calendar or check online at ⓦ www.honoluluweekly.com. The Gig List shows music by type (jazz, Hawaiian, rock/pop, etc....) and Spin Zone lists DJs and dancing.

Hanks Café ££ ⑭ Entertainment every night in this Chinatown gallery-turned-club. ⓐ 1038 Nuuanu Ave ⓣ 526 1410 ⓦ www.hankscafehonolulu.com ⓛ 13.00–02.00 daily

Jazz Minds ££ ⑮ Live jazz, food and drinks six nights a week – closed on Sundays. ⓐ 1661 Kapi`olani Bvd ⓣ 945 0800 ⓦ www.honolulujazzclub.com ⓛ 14.00–02.00 Mon–Sat

Lava Rock Lounge ££ ⑯ If you like what you hear as you walk through the International Marketplace, head upstairs for a drink. ⓐ 2330 Kalakaua Ave ⓣ 479 0335 ⓛ 19.00–04.00 Tues–Sun

Clubs

Art after Dark at the Honolulu Academy of Art ££ ⑰ Head here for live music, DJs, dancing. Gallery admission is included. ⓐ 900 South

Beretania St ☎ 532 8700 ⓦ www.artafterdark.org ⓛ Last Friday of each month

Pearl Ultralounge ££ ⑱ Enjoy DJ music from 22.30 at this stylish club. ⓐ Ho`okipa Terrace, 3rd floor, Ala Moana Center ☎ 944 8000 ⓦ www.pearlhawaii.com ⓛ 16.30–02.00 Mon–Thur, 16.30–04.00 Fri, 19.00–04.00 Sat

Señor Frog's ££ ⑲ Party until 04.00 with live music, karaoke and DJs. Full restaurant and bar. Part of the Royal Hawaiian Shopping Center. ⓐ 2201 Kalakaua Ave, Suite 313 ☎ 440 0150 ⓦ www.senorfrogs.com ⓛ 11.00–24.00 (restaurant); 11.00–04.00 (bar) daily

Thirtyninehotel ££ ⑳ Modern art and entertainment, there's always something different on show here. ⓐ 39 North Hotel ☎ 559 2552 ⓦ www.thirtyninehotel.com ⓛ 16.00–02.00 Tues–Sat

Venus Nightclub ££ ㉑ Head here for Las-Vegas-style revues, sexy theme nights and late-night dancing. ⓐ 1344 Kapi`olani Bvd ☎ 955 2640 ⓦ www.hawaiiscene.com/venus ⓛ Nightly till 04.00 (opening time varies according to event) ⓘ Admission charge and dress code

Oahu excursions

SOUTH OAHU

The Oahu coast becomes rugged and picturesque as you head south and east from Waikiki. The edge of Waikiki is marked by Diamond Head crater, a must-see sight for those with sturdy legs, and then the road hugs the coast past rugged cliffs and beaches where body surfers and day trippers from Waikiki get away from the crowds. If you're driving, you may end up sharing the road with cyclists pedalling their way around the island – give them plenty of room and your patience, they may be training for Hawaii's famous Ironman triathlon! South Oahu is home to some great snorkelling – try Hanauma Bay – and the windy shores are a favourite for kite fliers.

THINGS TO SEE & DO

Adventures from Koko Marina

The Koko Marina Shopping Center is home to a handful of commercial watersports excursion operators. Rent an underwater scooter that allows you to see below the waves without a scuba kit, book a surfing lesson, ride the 'duck' – a vehicle that goes from the beach into the water – take a fishing cruise...then dine in one of the marina's waterside restaurants.
ⓐ 7192 Kalanianaole Hwy ⓣ 395 4737
ⓦ www.kokomarinacenter.com/indexphp ⓛ Daily

Diamond Head

Climb 230 m (755 ft) above the south-east edge of Honolulu to look back at the skyscrapers and beaches of Waikiki. This 2.8-km (1¾-mile) hike includes 175 steps, but the views are worth it. Go early in the day to avoid the heat and the busloads of tour groups.

Hanauma Bay Nature Preserve

Hanauma Bay Nature Preserve is about 16 km (10 miles) south-east of Waikiki. It's not a watersports beach as such – there's no windsurfing or

● *Follow the Diamond Head trail for glittering views*

kayaking here – but there's excellent snorkelling. Arrive early if you're driving, as parking is limited. Snorkel kits are available for rent in the park. Because Hanauma Bay is a protected area, visitors are required to watch an introductory film about the formation of the bay and the resident sea life, and how to protect both yourself and the reef during your visit. There are fees for parking and entrance.

ⓐ 7455 Kalaniana`ole Hwy ⓣ 396 4229 ⓛ 06.00–18.00 Mon, Wed–Sun (Oct–Mar); 06.00–19.00 Sun & Mon, Wed–Fri, 06.00–22.00 Sat (Apr–Sept)

Sea Life Park

Swim with dolphins, visit sea lions, and watch penguin antics. There's a habitat area for the endangered Hawaiian monk seal, a sea turtle feeding pool, and opportunities to learn about the sea life of Hawaii and the Pacific. Call ahead if you want to swim with the dolphins, since reservations are required. There's an entrance fee for the park, and the dolphin swims cost extra.

ⓐ 41-202 Kalanianaole Hwy, #7, Waimanalo ⓣ 365 7446
ⓦ www.sealifeparkhawaii.com ⓛ 10.30–17.00 daily

TAKING A BREAK

Restaurants & bars

If you're not heading any further than Sea Life Park or the nearby beaches, you may find it most convenient to stock up on snacks or picnic supplies before leaving Waikiki. But if you're heading a little further up the island, continue along the highway until you reach Kailua, a town that has plenty of places in which you can get a cup of coffee or a bite to eat.

For fresh fruit and other edibles from local growers, check out the farmer's markets. Try the **People's Open Market** (ⓐ Kailua District Park, 21 South Kainalu Drive ⓣ 266 7652 ⓛ 09.00–10.00 Thur only).

Elvin's Bakery £ Pastries filled with local favourites – Portuguese sausage rolls, coconut pies, treats to take away.
ⓐ Kailua Shopping Center, 600 Kailua Rd ⓣ 262 1688 ⓛ 07.30–19.30 Mon–Fri, 08.00–19.00 Sat, 08.00–16.00 Sun

🔺 *The protected Hanauma Bay*

Lanikai Juice Company £ Fresh squeezed juice and yummy smoothies.
Ⓐ 600 Kailua Rd, #101 Ⓣ 262 2383 Ⓦ www.lanikaijuice.com
Ⓛ 06.00–20.00 Mon–Fri, 08.00–19.00 Sat & Sun

Morning Brew £ A popular morning gathering place for coffee and
light lunches. Ⓐ Kailua Shopping Center, 600 Kailua Rd, #119 Ⓣ 262 7770
Ⓦ www.morningbrewHawaii.com Ⓛ 06.00–20.00 daily

AFTER DARK

Baci Bistro ££ Casual European/Italian dining, fresh pasta made in
house, seafood, an extensive wine list. Ⓐ 30 Aulike St, Kailua Ⓣ 262 7555
Ⓦ www.bacibistro.com Ⓛ 11.30–22.00 Mon–Fri Ⓘ Reservations
recommended but not required

Boardrider's Bar and Grill ££ Beer on tap, casual dining, big-screen TVs,
pool tables and live, locally based entertainment. Ⓐ 201-A Hamakua
Drive, Kailua Ⓣ 261 4600 Ⓛ 11.00–02.00 daily Ⓘ Admission charge on
nights with live music

Buzz's Original Steak House ££ The name says it all. High-quality grilled
meats, some chicken and seafood and cocktails. Ⓐ 413 Kawailoa Rd,
Kailua Ⓐ 261 4661 Ⓛ 11.00–15.00 & 17.00–21.00 daily

Pinky's Pupu Bar and Grill ££ Beach-hut décor, burgers, seafood,
family-friendly dining. Full bar. Ⓐ 970 N Kalaheo Ave, Kailua Ⓣ 254 6255
Ⓛ 16.00–22.00 daily

Central & North Oahu

Oahu is small enough that you could combine any of the attractions listed below into a day trip to just about any other place on the island. The driving is easy, the distances manageable, and the beaches are always calling you – here you can take time to watch the surfers and admire the turquoise waters or jump in for a swim.

The shrimp trucks that line the road to the North Shore are a must for seafood lovers, or try a tropical fruit smoothie or a coffee milkshake. Take your time: you're never so far from your Waikiki hotel that you have to rush back. Pack your beach bag and luxuriate in the short distances and beautiful scenery.

THINGS TO SEE & DO

Dole Plantation

In 1901, James Dole planted pineapple in Wahiawa, going on to such great success that he was known as the Pineapple King. Visit the plantation to learn about how the fruit is cultivated, tour the gardens, get lost in a giant maze and ride the Pineapple Express train. The visitor's centre has a gift shop and restaurant where you can purchase pineapple treats and souvenirs and watch a pineapple-cutting demonstration. In the courtyards, craftspeople sell Hawaiian-made jewellery, *leis*, candles and other handicrafts. The visitor's centre is open to all. Admission charge for the gardens, the maze and the train ride.

ⓐ 64-1550 Kamehameha Hwy, Wahiawa ⓣ 621 8408
ⓦ www.dole-plantation.com ⓛ 09.00–17.30 daily

Hale`iwa

This funky beach town on Oahu's North Shore offers a striking contrast to the glitzy shopping and high-rise hotels back in Waikiki. The Triple Crown of Surfing takes place here for a reason – legendary waves and wide sandy beaches have been drawing surfers to Hale`iwa from around the world for years.

● *Pineapples aplenty at Dole Plantation*

The town of Hale`iwa reflects that 'hang loose' surfing attitude. Brightly painted plantation-era buildings nowadays contain a range of restaurants, galleries and beach and surf shops. Surfboard rentals and surfing schools are plentiful. If you want to hear about the golden days of surfing, drop in at the Hale`iwa Surf Museum for a chat with the proprietor.

ⓐ 66-250 Kamehameha Hwy ❶ 637 3406

Pali Lookout

View Oahu from this windy ridge overlooking the Koolau Mountain Range. In 1795 King Kamehameha and his warriors sent his opposition over these steep, forested cliffs and went on to unite the Hawaiian Islands. For the Nu`uanu Pali Drive, follow the signs to the Lookout.

Polynesian Cultural Center

This cultural amusement park showcases the people of Hawaii, Samoa, Maori New Zealand, Fiji, Tahiti, the Marquesas and Tonga. Packages include a whole range of options: a canoe pageant, an evening *lu`au*, a tram tour, an IMAX movie, even transportation from your hotel. The park offers variety of places to get lunch or snacks – in addition to the *lu`au* meals – and, of course, a gift shop. Book online for discounted prices.

ⓐ 55-370 Kamehameha Hwy, La`ie ⓣ 293 3333 ⓦ http://polynesia.com ⓛ 12.00–18.30 daily (*lu`au* hours vary)

TAKING A BREAK

Matsumoto's Shave Ice £ Queue alongside the locals to get a giant cone of 'shave ice' – don't call it shaved ice – topped with sweet fruit juice or syrup. ⓐ 66-087 Kamehameha Hwy ⓣ 637 4827 ⓦ www.matsumotoshaveice.com ⓛ 08.30–18.00 daily

🔺 *Enjoy local dancing at the Polynesian Cultural Center*

Ted's Bakery £ Locally famous chocolate *haupia* pie – a chocolate and coconut pudding confection. Go straight to dessert or try a bento box – chicken or beef, plenty of rice and sauce. ⓐ 59-024 Kamehameha Hwy ⓣ 638 8207 ⓛ 07.00–18.00 daily

Shrimp Trucks ££ Heading north on the east side of Oahu, you can't miss the shrimp trucks by the side of the road. Try the Shrimp Shack parked outside Kaya's store in Punalu`u or Giovanni's Aloha Shrimp Truck in Kahuku – or any one of them where you see people queuing up outside! ⓐ Kamehameha Hwy ⓣ 293 9095 ⓛ Daily

AFTER DARK

Hale`iwa Joe's ££ Full meals or smaller plates, fresh seafood with the bonus of a big outdoor patio to enjoy it all on. ⓐ 66-011 Kamehameha Hwy ⓣ 637 8005 ⓦ www.haleiwajoes.com/locations-haleiwa.html ⓛ Lunch & dinner daily

Jameson's by the Sea ££ Ocean views and fresh seafood, with a mellow North Shore vibe. ⓐ 62-540 Kamehameha Hwy ⓣ 637 6272 ⓦ www.jamesonshawaii.com/jamesonshaleiwa.htm ⓛ 11.00–21.30 Mon–Fri, 09.00–21.30 Sat & Sun

The Kona & Kohala Coasts

As your flight lands at Kona International Airport at Keahole, it's hard to imagine that, in the midst of all that black lava, there are spectacular beaches, protected coves and an endless variety of resort options. On Hawai`i, known as the Big Island, you'll find a diverse range of ecosystems, from active volcanic peaks to sparkling beaches.

Kailua-Kona is the centre for shopping and nightlife. It is a lovely beach village, with a farmer's market, beachwear and souvenir shops, and restaurants with outdoor seating facing the sunset. Hotels, apartments and holiday rental places line Ali`i Drive from Kailua-Kona to Keahou Bay.

North of the Kona airport on the Kohala Coast the resorts are further apart and a little more secluded than those on the Kona Coast. The coastline is a little more rugged here, but there are plenty of splendid beaches. You'll have that 'getting away from it all' feeling in a surprisingly short time. The nearest 'city' is still Kailua-Kona, to the south of the airport.

BEACHES

West Hawai`i is the resort centre for a reason – excellent beaches line the coast. Some are places in which to see sea turtles or to go snorkelling; others have active surf and are best for sports; still others offer sheltered bays and parks where kids can swim and play.

Anaeho`omal`u Beach
Also known as A-Bay, this provides excellent swimming and sunbathing and is popular at weekends. Drive north from Kailua-Kona to the Outrigger Waikoloa Beach Resort, then follow the signs for parking and beach access. ⓐ Marriott Waikoloa Beach Resort, north of Kailua-Kona

Kahalu`u Beach Park
Excellent snorkelling in clear waters at the south end of the beach, body boarding and surfing at the north end. Facilities here include public toilets, showers, a lifeguard tower and limited parking.

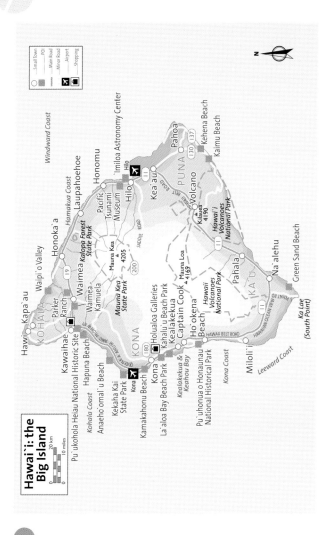

🔺 *A green turtle basking on lava rocks*

Kamkahonu Beach

Between the Kailua-Kona Pier and the King Kamehameha Hotel on Ali`i Drive. A calm surf makes this a great swimming beach for children. Good snorkelling for stronger swimmers. Rent water toys – snorkel gear, kayaks – at concession stalls nearby.

Kekaha Kai State Park

Pretty and quiet, with limited facilities – just picnic tables under coconut trees and a few outhouses. Situated just north of the Kona International Airport – look for the sign on the highway.

La`aloa Bay Beach Park

Also called White Sands, Magic Sands or Disappearing Sands Beach Park. In winter, waves wash away the beach; when the beach is 'in', you'll see body boarders and surfers in the water and beach volleyball being played on the sand. Good whale watching in season. There are public conveniences, showers and lifeguards. 🅰 Ali`i Drive, just south of Kailua-Kona

THINGS TO SEE & DO

Holualoa Galleries & Cafés

Coffee fields and dense greenery surround this artist's village just ten minutes' drive from Kailua-Kona. Browse the work of local painters, sculptors, jewellers and ukulele makers. The town hosts a 'Coffee & Art Stroll', with exhibitors showing off their wares, plus food vendors and entertainment. Tour a coffee plantation and then settle in at one of the town's little cafés to enjoy a cup of the local brew.

Kailua-Kona Village

Restaurants, shopping, galleries and nightlife are all centred in this beach village. Visit **King Kalakaua's Summer Palace** to see artefacts from the Hawaiian monarchy or to hear live Hawaiian music. (Note that the palace was damaged by an earthquake in 2006 and some of the rooms may not be accessible.) **Moku`aikaua Church** is Hawaii's oldest Christian church. The lobby of **King Kamehameha's Kona Beach Hotel** has murals that portray 18th-century Hawaiian life. There's a lively farmer's market that takes place from Thursday to Saturday – pick up a brightly coloured wrap or a bunch of beautiful flowers.

Pu`ukohola Heiau National Historic Site

This site is home to three *heiau*, or temples, built by King Kamehameha I. One of the temples was built in response to a prophecy that the builder would become king of a unified Hawaii. When Kamehameha's rival was killed on this site, the king went on to unify the Hawaiian Islands. Only two of the temples are visible today – one is submerged under the waters of Pelekane Bay. John Young, a sailor who went on to become one of the king's trusted advisors, also had his homestead at this site.
The visitor's centre has displays about native Hawaiian culture and the local wildlife. Take the trail down to the very pretty beach and keep your eyes on the water for black-tipped reef sharks!
ⓐ 62-3601 Kawaihae Rd ⓣ 974 6200 ⓦ www.nps.gov/puhe/
ⓗ 07.30–16.00 daily

TAKING A BREAK

Kailua-Kona

Killer Tacos Incorporated £ Fresh, fast Mexican food, north of Kailua-Kona village. ⓐ 74-5483 Kaiwi St ⓣ 329 3335 ⓦ www.killertacos.com ⓛ 10.00–21.00 daily

L&L Hawaiian BBQ £ Traditional 'plate lunches' (meat with rice and macaroni salad) and local specialities. The chain has branches in lots of different locations, providing fast and cheap food. ⓐ 76-6831 Ali`i Drive, Suite D-124 (Keauhou Shopping Center) ⓣ 322 9888 ⓦ www.hawaiianbarbecue.com ⓛ 07.00–20.00 daily

Lava Java £ Bistro-style food, breakfast, lunch and dinner. Also serves excellent coffee milkshakes. ⓐ 75-5799 Ali`i Drive ⓣ 327 2161 ⓦ www.islandlavajavakona.com ⓛ 06.00–22.00 daily

● *A traditional outrigger canoe on the South Kona coast*

Sweet Ohana Candy Factory £ You can't miss the big pink building just up the hill in Kona Village. Local food, American-style diner meals, 'candy' made on site. ⓐ 75 Ali'i Drive ⓣ 329 7696 ⓦ www.sweetohanacandy.com ⓛ 07.00–18.00 Tue–Sun, closed Mon

Kawaihae (near Pu`ukohola National Historic Site)
Kawaihae Market and Deli £ A small market that provides takeaway snacks and some freshly prepared items. ⓐ Kawaihae Shopping Center ⓣ 880 1611 ⓛ 04.30–21.00 Mon–Fri, 05.30–20.00 Sat & Sun

Café Pesto ££ Serves pizza and salads. ⓐ Kawaihae Shopping Center ⓣ 882 1071 ⓛ 11.00–21.00 Sun–Thur, 11.00–22.00 Fri & Sat

AFTER DARK

Kailua-Kona/Kohala Coast
Fujimamas ££ Sushi, tempura and Japanese-style entrées amid attractive South Asian décor. ⓐ 75-5719 Ali'i Drive ⓣ 327 2125 ⓛ 11.30–14.00 Mon–Sat & 17.00–22.00 daily

Huggo's ££ Fresh seafood, beautiful waterfront views and tropical cocktails. Located at the southern end of Kailua-Kona Village. ⓐ 75-5828 Kahakai Rd ⓣ 329 1493 ⓦ www.huggos.com ⓛ 11.30–14.30 Mon–Fri, 17.30–22.00 Sat & Sun

Kona Brewing Company ££ Kona brewed beer, a garden lit by flaming tiki torches and plenty of good bar food. ⓐ 75-5629 Kuakini Highway ⓣ 334 2739 ⓦ www.konabrewingco.com ⓛ 11.00–22.00 Sun–Thur, 11.00–23.00 Fri & Sat

Royal Thai Cafe ££ Delicious, affordable Thai food in the Keauhou Shopping Center. ⓐ 78-6831 Ali'i Drive (Keauhou Shopping Center) ⓣ 322 8424 ⓛ 11.00–22.00 daily

Hualalai Grill £££ Hawaii Regional Cuisine (see page 96) in an open-air restaurant overlooking the resort gardens. ⓐ At the Hualalai Resort ⓣ 325 8525 ⓦ www.hualalairesort.com ⓛ 11.30–14.20 & 17.30–21.00 daily

Sunset cruises
Blue Sea Cruises ££ Dinner, drinks and entertainment – plus after-dark viewing of sea life through the glass-bottomed wells in the hull. Children over eight are welcome. ⓐ Kailua-Kona Pier ⓣ 331 8875 ⓦ www.blueseacruisesinc.com ⓛ 17.00–21.00 daily

Body Glove Adults Only Sunset Sail ££ Two hours of live music, an open bar and pupu platters (plates of American-Chinese appetisers). ⓐ Kailua-Kona Pier ⓣ 326 7122 ⓛ 17.00–19.30 Wed & Fri

Captain Bean's Dinner Cruise ££ A two-hour cruise of the Kona waters with live music, buffet dinner and bar (one drink included in the price). ⓐ Kailua-Kona Pier ⓛ 16.50–19.15 Thur–Sun

Clubs
Hard Rock Café ££ Just as you find elsewhere on the planet, with lots of celebrity kitsch, stiff drinks, loud music, and a lively party scene. ⓐ 75-5815 Ali`i Drive ⓣ 329 8866 ⓛ 11.00–23.00 daily

Huggo's on the Rocks ££ Right next door to the restaurant of the same name, but with a younger crowd, dancing – and lighter meals on the menu. ⓐ 75-5828 Kahakai Rd ⓣ 329 1493 ⓦ www.huggos.com ⓛ 11 30 until closing daily

Lulu's ££ Oceanside, open air, DJs and dancing until about 01.30. ⓐ 75-5819 Ali`i Drive ⓣ 331 2633 ⓦ www.lulushawaii.com ⓛ Until 01.30 daily

Lu`aus

Kona Village Resort *Lu`au* **££** Traditionally prepared Hawaiian foods and a romantic setting under the palms. ⓐ Queen Kaahumanu Hwy ⓣ 325 5555 ⓦ www.konavillage.com ⓒ 18.00–21.00 Wed & Fri

Legends of the Pacific ££ Exotic Polynesian dances and music of the Pacific Rim at the Hilton Waikoloa Village. ⓐ 425 Waikoloa Beach Drive ⓣ 886 1234 ⓦ www.hiltonwaikoloavillage.com ⓒ 17.30–21.00 Tues & Fri

Island Breeze *Lu`au* **£££** Outdoors and on the beach at the King Kamehameha's Kona Beach Hotel. Cocktail and dinner shows. ⓐ 74-5599 Luhia St ⓣ 329 8111 ⓦ www.islandbreezeluau.com ⓒ 17.30–21.00 Sun, Tues–Fri

Lava, Legends & Legacies £££ A tour of the islands through dance and song at the Royal Kona Resort. ⓐ 75-5852 Ali'i Drive, ⓣ 329 3111 ⓦ www.hawaiihotels.com ⓒ 17.00 Mon, Wed & Fri

Big Island excursions

SOUTH KONA
Pu`uhonua o Honaunau National Historical Park

During Hawai`i's time of strict *kapu*, or law, punishment for those offending the royal classes was swift and fatal. If you'd offended the chief, you had one option only – seek refuge, and fast – in the *pu`uhonua*, or place of refuge. This spectacular site, under coconut palms and on the edge of a protected bay, still offers a feeling of peaceful sanctuary, in spite of the vast numbers of tourists who come here to see it.

The visitor's centre has an open-air theatre and interpretative displays that present the culture and history of the site. Wander the grounds to see the *Ki`i* – carved wooden statues – and the former resting place of Hawaiian chiefs. Keone`ele Cove is visited by sea turtles: you'll see them swimming in the sheltered water or taking a beach break.

There's a picnic area in the park and good snorkelling area just north at **Honaunau Bay**. Plan to spend half a day here, longer if you want to go snorkelling after you've visited the park. Bring food, as there are no eating places in the park. Bottled water is available at the visitor's centre and there is also a drinking fountain.

Kealakekua Bay

The clear sheltered waters and limited number of tour operators here make Kealakekua Bay a snorkeller's oasis. Strong arms can kayak from Kealakekua Harbor, strong legs can walk from the town of Captain Cook – but be warned, it's a steep return on a rough track. Perhaps the best way to arrive is by the *Fair Winds II*: the Fair Wind company operates snorkel cruises to this cove. No matter how you arrive, this is a must-visit stop for snorkellers – the clear visibility, warm waters, near absence of surf and variety of marine life provides some of the island's best fish viewing.

On shore there's a monument to Captain Cook, the explorer given credit for 'discovering' Hawai`i centuries after the Polynesian navigators made it their home. Captain Cook had the good fortune to land in

Kealakekua Bay during a festival that prohibited the Hawaiian people from engaging in any kind of conflict. Cook and his men basked in hospitality, plundered native resources, and set sail again, thinking that the people they'd met were the most passive and generous on the planet. When Cook's crew landed again after the festival was over, they learned otherwise, and Cook and many of his crew were killed. The monument marks the site of his death.

Fair Wind Big Island Ocean Guides 🅰 78-7130 Kaleiopapa St, Kailua-Kona 📞 345 0268 🅦 www.fair-wind.com 🅘 Reservations required, particularly in high season

TAKING A BREAK

The Coffee Shack £ A mile south of the Captain Cook post office, the owners of the Coffee Shack grow their beans right below the balcony where you'll drink it. Great views, American breakfasts, sandwiches and pizza. 🅰 83-5799 Mamalahoa Hwy 📞 328 9555 🅦 www.coffeeshack.com 🕐 07.30–15.00 daily

Manago Hotel Restaurant £ No-frills food at affordable prices. Famous for its pork chops. 🅰 82-6155 Mamalahoa Hwy 📞 323 2642 🅦 www.managohotel.com 🕐 07.00–21.00 Tues–Sun

South Kona Fruit Stand £ Located on the Mamalahoa Highway between mile markers 103 and 104. Exotic produce, locally grown snacks and delicious smoothies. 🅰 Mamalahoa Hwy 📞 No phone 🕐 08.00–17.00 Mon–Fri, 09.00–18.00 Sat & Sun

HAWAI`I VOLCANOES NATIONAL PARK

Breaks in the earth's crust release sulphurous steam into the air. Crater walls are lined with bright yellow mineral deposits. And sometimes you'll see hot lava pouring out of the ground into the sea. A trip to Hawai`i Volcanoes National Park brings home very clearly the fact that Hawai`i is an active volcano.

Be aware that it can be sunny and dry at your hotel but pouring with rain and cool at Volcanoes National Park. Even if it's not raining, clouds often cloak the slopes of the volcano, obscuring visibility. Don't let the weather deter you – the park is worth a visit, rain or shine, with fog and clouds adding a mysterious air to the environment. Make sure you've got a full tank of petrol, though – there's none available in the park.

Day hikes and overnight wilderness adventures are available in the park. There's also a camping ground, a lodge, a visitor's centre, a gallery and a museum. The museum displays – focused on geology and volcano research – are a little tired, but kids love jumping up and down in front of the seismometer, a device that measures movements in the earth.

Chain of Craters Road
Before you head down, ask a park ranger if the lava floe is active and accessible, so you won't be disappointed.

◠ *A lava lightshow at Hawai`i Volcanoes National Park*

Crater Rim Drive

The road winds through several different ecosystems and has lots of scenic viewpoints and short walks. Walk through the Thurston Lava Tube beforehand – the dense rainforest makes a striking contrast to the bare landscape of the caldera.

TAKING A BREAK

In the park

Volcano House Hotel ££ This is the only place in the park that sells food. Get a quick bite from the snack bar or a full meal in the restaurant. Visit the lounge for signature cocktails with volcano-inspired names. It is located across the street from the Kilauea Visitor Center and on the rim of Kilauea Caldera. ⓐ Volcanoes National Park ☎ 967 7321 ⓦ www.volcanohousehotel.com 🕐 07.00–10.30, 11.00–14.00 & 17.30–21.00 daily

Outside the park

Kiawe Kitchen ££ Home-style Italian food, seafood and pizza from the wood-fired oven. The food here is really good. ⓐ 19-4005 Haunani Rd ☎ 967 7711 🕐 12.00–14.30 & 17.30–21.30 daily

Thai Thai Restaurant ££ Thai hot means really hot – be sure to let your waiter or waitress know if you don't want your food too spicy. ⓐ 19-4084 Volcano Rd ☎ 967 7969 🕐 09.00–21.00 daily

Kilauea Lodge and Restaurant £££ Conveniently situated for visitors to the park. New menus nightly. ⓐ 19-3948 Old Volcano Rd ☎ 967 7366 ⓦ www.kilauea.com 🕐 17.30–22.00 daily

HILO

This town on Hawai`i's eastern side doesn't get much attention from visitors. There are few places to stay and the downtown is a funky mishmash of tiny ethnic restaurants, second-hand and souvenir shops.

🔺 *Getting away from the crowds near Hilo*

That's the appeal – it's a change from the groomed lawns and shiny exteriors of the resort areas in West Hawai`i. If you're looking for modern Hawaiian life beyond the hotels, you'll find it in Hilo.

THINGS TO SEE & DO

`Imiloa Astronomy Center of Hawai`i

The striking `Imiloa Astronomy Center plays architectural homage to Hawai`i's volcanoes, but it's more than elegant architecture. The centre educates visitors about the link between Hawaiian culture and the stars – the Polynesians used the stars to navigate the Pacific before Europe's explorers sailed the high seas. There is also a planetarium, lots of hands-on exhibits and a café. Give yourself an hour and a half, minimum, so you can catch a planetarium show. ⓐ 600 `Imiloa Place ① 969 9700 ⓦ www.imiloahawaii.org ⓛ 10.00–16.00 Tues–Sat ① Admission charge

Pacific Tsunami Museum

Downtown Hilo has a slightly weary look for a reason. The oceanside town was hit by a tsunami in 1946 and again in 1960. The Pacific Tsunami Museum provides maps to self-guided walking and driving tours of sites affected by those giant tidal waves – and the museum devotes more resources to tsunami education.

ⓐ 130 Kamehameha Ave ⓣ 935 0926 ⓦ www.tsunami.org
ⓛ 09.00–16.00 Mon–Sat ⓘ Admission charge

TAKING A BREAK

Farmer's market £ Try a Spam and egg *musibi* (rice, nori and Spam), pick up a fresh noodle dish, and wash it all down with passion fruit drink.
ⓐ At the corner of Mamo St & Kamehameha Ave in downtown Hilo
ⓛ Wed & Sat

⬤ *Reach for the stars at `Imiloa Astronomy Center*

Hilo Bay Sugar Shack £ Adventurous? Try the *halo halo*, a Filipino dessert speciality, made from sweet preserved beans and tropical fruits, and topped with ice cream. Right next door to the farmer's market.
🄰 Mamo St, Kamehameha Ave 🄣 933 1000
🅦 www.hilofarmersmarket.com 🄫 07.00–15.00 Wed & Sat
Mamo Street market 🄫 08.00–17.00 daily

Big Island Pizza ££ Exotic variety of topics on thick crust pizza.
🄰 760 Kilauea Ave 🄣 934 8000 🅦 www.bigislandpizza.com
🄫 11.00–21.00 daily

Hilo Bay Café ££ Tricky to find but worth the bother. Seafood, generous salads. 🄰 315 Makaala St, #109 🄣 935 4939 🅦 www.hilobaycafe.com
🄫 11.00–21.00 Mon–Sat

⬤ *Verdant foliage at Hilo's Rainbow Falls*

AFTER DARK

Restaurants

Harrington's Restaurant £££ Steak and seafood with a view of Reed's Bay.
ⓐ 135 Kalanianaole Ave ❶ 961 4966 ❶ 11.00–16.00 Mon–Fri, 13.00–21.00 daily ❶ Reservations recommended

Seaside Restaurant £££ Fresh seafood lunch or dinner.
ⓐ 1790 Kalanianaole Ave ❶ 935 8825 ⓦ www.seasiderestaurant.com
❶ 17.00–20.30 Tues–Thur, 17.00–21.00 Fri & Sat

Clubs

Flipside Too £ A rowdy party bar with big, cheap drinks. Call a cab.
ⓐ 94 Mamo St ❶ 961 0057 ❶ 19.00–04.00 daily

**Ho`omalimali Lounge £** Dancing and live music on Friday and Saturday nights at the Hawai`i Naniloa Resort. ⓐ 93 Banyan Drive ❶ 969 3333
❶ 21.00–24.00 Fri & Sat

THE HAMAKUA COAST

The windward side of the island has steep cliffs and more rain than the west side. The rain brings more green – and good farming. The cliffs earn the Hamakua Coast its 'Waterfall Country' nickname. Sugar was the main crop here until the 1990s; now there are some attempts to bring agritourism to the region.

Waipi`o Valley

The biggest draw along the Hamakua Coast is the stopped-in-time Waipi`o Valley. The land in the valley is privately owned and facilities are extremely limited – no phones, no electricity, and not much by way of roads. Local boys head down on their overloaded ATVs, lugging body boards to the black sand beach, but don't be tempted to do the same. The Waipi`o Valley is open only to guided tours and those on overnight backpacking trips. You'll need to book a tour if you want to visit.

THINGS TO SEE & DO

Horseback & walking tours of the valley begin by taking you down the steep road in a 4WD vehicle. Then you'll pass through a patchwork of bright green taro patches crisscrossed with irrigation streams, and through lush dense rainforest.

Na`alapa Stables Saddle up with the *paniolos* (Hawaiian cowboys) in the valley for a 1½- or 2-hour ride on this 12,000 acre working ranch. Groups are kept small – ten riders maximum. Children over eight years old are welcome.
ⓐ Kahua Ranch Hwy 250 ⓣ 775 0419
ⓦ www.naalapastables.com ⓛ 09.00–11.30 & 13.30–15.00 daily

Waipi`o Valley Wagon Tours Mule carriages, storytelling and history.
ⓐ Who Ranch Hwy 240 ⓣ 775 9518 ⓦ www.waipiovalleywagontours.com
ⓛ 10.30, 12.30 & 14.30 Mon–Sat

TAKING A BREAK

If you're not taking a tour, stop at the viewpoint above the Waipi`o Valley. You'll see the black sand beach and the bright green patches of taro, the Hawaiian root crop. Park rangers at the top of the road into the valley can answer any questions that hikers heading for the camping ground in the next valley might have.

Cafés & restaurants
Café Rendezvous £ Serves a range of sweet and savoury crêpes, coffee, ginger ice tea. ⓐ 45-3490 Mamane St ⓣ 775 9230 ⓛ 10.00–16.00 Tues–Thur, 10.00–17.00 Fri, 10.00–14.00 Sat

Simply Natural £ Healthfood store and café with pancakes for breakfast and sandwiches for lunch. ⓐ Hwy 240, Honoka`a ⓣ 775-0119 ⓛ 09.00–16.00 Mon–Sat

◯ *On top of the world: the Mauna Kea Observatory*

Tex Drive-in & Restaurant £ Fresh *malasadas* (doughnuts) and local food. Popular with locals. 🚋 45-690 Pakalana ☎ 775 0598 🌐 www.texdrivein.com 🕒 06.00–20.30 daily ❶ Cash only

Café Il Mondo ££ Stone-oven-baked pizza accompanied by occasional live acoustic guitar music from the owner. 🚋 45-3626 Mamane St, #A ☎ 775 7711 🕒 11.00–21.00 Mon–Sat

UPCOUNTRY & MAUNA KEA

The land between Hawai`i's two volcanoes, Mauna Kea and Mauna Loa, is cattle country. Parker Ranch, established 150 years ago, is still one of the world's largest cattle ranches. The countryside around Waimea maintains the Western tradition of a culture centred around the *paniolo*, the Hawaiian cowboy.

THINGS TO SEE & DO

Mauna Kea Observatory

Above Waimea, at 4,200 m (13,780 ft), sits the Mauna Kea Observatory. The visitor's centre is an hour's drive from Waimea – you'll need a 4WD vehicle if you want to go all the way to the observatory. There are daily guided tours to the summit, but you'll have to provide your own transportation. Your best bet may be to book a stargazing tour where your transportation, the warm clothing you need to handle the difference in temperature at such a high elevation, and even, in some cases, a gourmet picnic dinner, are provided.

Mauna Kea Visitor Information Station 🚋 Mauna Kea Access Rd ☎ 935 6268 🌐 www.ifa.Hawaii.edu/info/vis 🕒 09.00–22.00 daily

Parker Ranch Museum & Visitor Center

Horse-riding tours leave regularly from Parker Ranch, one of the largest and oldest ranches in the United States. If you're not keen to get in the saddle, there are wagon rides – or you can explore the ranch's historical homes. Parker Ranch isn't the only show in town – other properties also offer riding, ATV tours, and host 'paniolo nights' – barbecue dinners with music, storytelling and stargazing.

ⓐ 67-1435 Mamalahoa Hwy, Kamuela ⓣ 885 7655
ⓦ www.parkerranch.com ⓛ 09.00–17.00 Mon–Sat

TAKING A BREAK

Cafés & restaurants

Waimea Coffee Company £ A lovely little café and shop with Hawaiian-grown coffees and souvenirs. ⓐ 63-1279 Kawaihae Rd, #114 ⓣ 885 4472
ⓦ www.waimeacoffeecompany.com ⓛ 07.00–17.00 Mon–Fri, 08.00–16.00 Sat

Hawaiian Style Café ££ More of a diner than a café, serving good food – a proper local favourite. Breakfast and lunch only. ⓐ 64-1290 Mamalahoa Hwy ⓣ 885 4295 ⓛ 06.00–13.00 Mon–Sat, 07.00–11.00 Sun

Huli Sue's BBQ & Grill ££ Big servings of curry, chilli – and grilling after 17.00. ⓐ 64-957 Mamalahoa Hwy ⓣ 885 6268 ⓦ www.hulisues.com
ⓛ 11.30–20.30 Mon–Sat

AFTER DARK

Daniel Thiebaut £££ Serving up French-Asian cuisine, lots of fresh seafood and great family brunches. ⓐ 65-1259 Kawaihae Rd ⓣ 887 2200
ⓦ www.danielthiebaut.com ⓛ 09.00–21.00 daily

Merriman's £££ Famous for some of the best food in the islands, using seasonal and local produce. ⓐ Opelo Plaza, Hwy 19 & Opelo Rd
ⓣ 885 6822 ⓦ www.merrimanshawaii.com ⓛ 11.30–13.30 & 17.30–21.00 Mon–Fri, 17.30–21.00 Sat & Sun ⓘ Reservations required

Po`ipu

Situated on Kauai, an island renowned for its stunning natural scenery, Po`ipu is a fast-expanding resort area. It offers just about any kind of accommodation you can imagine, from luxurious hotels with complicated swimming pools to little beach cottages and fully appointed holiday homes – and none of them are far from the sand. Po`ipu is something of a resort boomtown – expect to see even more choices over the next couple of years. It's popular for a reason: the beaches are lovely, the snorkelling is excellent and the location – close to shopping and the airport in nearby Lihu`e – makes it an easy first choice for visitors to Kauai. As a resort town, most of the dining and snack stops are in the hotels, but little Koloa, just up the road, has restaurants and shopping, too, though South Kauai beats it for convenience and variety.

BEACHES

Po`ipu Beach Park

A wide sandy beach, within walking distance of most Po`ipu hotels and resorts. Safe for children and a favourite of monk seals. There's good snorkelling and swimming and there are lifeguards too.

Prince Kuhio Beach Park

A small curve of beach that is popular with snorkellers and surfers. It is best for watersports; it's not a great sunbathing spot. Parking is limited, so it's best to walk if you're close. There are public toilets here.

Salt Pond Beach Park

On the site of former salt collection ponds. A protected cove with good snorkelling and swimming and excellent windsurfing, the outside reef makes it dangerous for surfers. The beach has public toilets, showers and lifeguards.

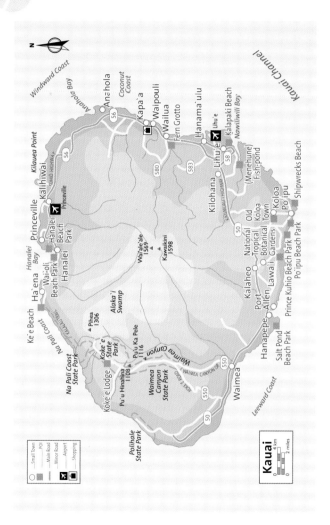

Shipwrecks Beach

Located in front of the Hyatt on the east end of the Po`ipu resort area, this beach is good for walks and body boarding. The surf is rough, though, so it's not good for children or inexperienced swimmers. There's parking, showers and public conveniences.

THINGS TO SEE & DO

National Tropical Botanical Gardens

Start your visit at the visitor's centre across from Spouting Horn in Po`ipu. There's a display garden and you can book your shuttle to the McBryde Garden or the Allerton Garden. The Allerton Garden was once a retreat for Hawaii's Queen Emma and remains a place that blends formal and wild beauty. The McBryde Garden covers a variety of ecosystems and is home to waterfalls, flowering trees and a state-of-the-art horticultural facility. Allow 2½ hours for the Allerton Garden, 1½ hours for the McBryde Garden.

Tours run regularly and reservations aren't required. A warning – there are lots of biting insects in the gardens, even at the visitor's centre. Wear mosquito repellent.

ⓐ 4425 Lawa`i Rd ⓣ 742 2623 ⓦ www.ntbg.org ⓛ 08.30–17.00 daily ⓘ Admission charge

Old Koloa Town

Hawaii's first sugar plantation was built in 1830 near current-day Koloa. Plantation-era buildings line the streets, but instead of housing farm workers and sugar offices, they're home to souvenir shops and restaurants. The History Center, behind the main business street, showcases plantation-era life. Koloa's lovely little downtown area is a fun stop for browsing and getting a casual meal – you may find yourself here more than once because of the convenient location on the road to Po`ipu.

Koloa History Center Building ⓐ Off Koloa Rd ⓦ www.oldkoloa.com ⓛ 09.00–21.00 daily

TAKING A BREAK

Lappert's Ice Cream £ Available all over Hawaii but the business was
founded in Kauai. Delicious scoops: try the Kona Coffee or the Kauai Pie.
ⓐ 5242 Koloa Rd ❶ 356 4045 Ⓦ www.lappertshawaii.com
🕐 09.00–21.00 daily

Pizzetta ££ Pizza and salads, casual sports bar environment.
Excellent pizza, friendly service. ⓐ 5408 Koloa Rd ❶ 742 8881
Ⓦ www.pizzettarestaurant.com 🕐 11.00–21.00 Mon–Fri, 11.00–22.00
Sat & Sun

AFTER DARK

Restaurants
Keoki's Paradise ££ Go here for seafood specialities and the famous Hula
Pie ice-cream dessert. Live Hawaiian music from Monday to Friday.
ⓐ 2360 Kiahuna Plantation Drive ❶ 742 7534
Ⓦ www.keokisparadise.com 🕐 11.00–22.00 daily

The Point ££ At the Sheraton Kauai Resort, sip cocktails while enjoying
spectacular sunsets. The menu is light – sandwiches, salads and pizzas –
and there's live music and dancing from Thursday to Saturday. ⓐ 2440
Hoonani Rd ❶ 742 1661 Ⓦ www.sheraton-kauai.com 🕐 11.00–24.00 daily

Roy's Bar and Grill ££ Hawaiian fusion cuisine by well-known Hawaiian
chef Roy Yamaguchi. ⓐ 2360 Kiahuna Plantation Drive ❶ 742 5000
Ⓦ www.roysrestaurant.com 🕐 17.30–22.00 daily ❗ Reservations
recommended

Yum Cha at the Grand Hyatt Resort ££ Presents Asian fusion cuisine and
a variety of wine, sakes and tea. ⓐ 1571 Po`ipu Rd ❶ 742 1515
Ⓦ www.grandhyatt.com 🕐 17.00–21.00 Tues–Sat
❗ Reservations required

Bar

Stevenson's Library ££ Enjoy cocktails and jazz in the elegant wood-panelled bar of the Grand Hyatt. There is a dress code.
ⓐ 1571 Po`ipu Rd ⓣ 742 1234 ⓦ www.kauai.hyatt.com
ⓛ 18.00–24.00 daily

Lu`aus

Havaiki Nui at the Grand Hyatt Resort ££ Listen for the conch shell signalling the start of an evening of festivities. Tropical drinks, traditional Hawaiian cuisine and amazing songs and dances from the Polynesian Islands. ⓐ 1571 Po`ipu Rd ⓣ 742 1234 ⓦ www.grandhyattkauailuau.com
ⓛ 17.45–20.00 Thur & Sun

**Surf to Sunset *Lu`au* at the Sheraton Kauai ££** Alongside Po`ipu Beach, this evening serves up entertainment and an extensive menu. Hawaiian artisans display traditional handicrafts before the show.
ⓐ 2440 Hoonani Rd ⓣ 742 8200 ⓦ www.sheraton-kauai.com
ⓛ 17.00 Mon & Fri

North Shore resorts: Princeville & Hanalei

Princeville's upmarket properties and well-groomed golf courses take visitors away from it all while being close to Hanalei's gorgeous beach, shopping and surf town vibe. This planned community used to be a coffee plantation, but now it boasts restaurants and luxury holiday homes. Around Hanalei are a handful of smaller hotels and beach cottages.

BEACHES

Hanalei Beach Park & Wai`oli Beach Park

These two parks are popular with both surfers and sunbathers. Ask the lifeguards about swimming conditions before you venture in. The parks have public toilets, lifeguards, picnic facilities and showers.

Ke`e Beach

Located at the end of the road on the north-east side of Kauai. There is good snorkelling to be had here, plus views of the Na Pali Coast. The parking spaces fill up early because the car park is also used by hikers on the Kalalau Trail. Limited facilities.

THINGS TO SEE & DO

The Princeville and Hanalei resorts are especially close to the Na Pali Coast and a number of natural preserves (see pages 62 and 65 for more information).

TAKING A BREAK

Java Kai £ Serves biscuits, smoothies, good coffee and lots of healthy treats. ③ 5-5183C Kuhio Hwy ① 826 6717 ① 06.30–18.00 daily

Polynesia Café ££ Casual dining – sandwiches, tacos, grilled fish – and outdoor seating in the centre of Hanalei. This is also a popular

⏷ *The lush and dramatic coastline of Kauai, the 'Garden Isle'*

after-dark destination with live music. ⓐ 5300 Ka Haku Rd ⓣ 826 1999 ⓛ 08.00–21.00 daily

Postcards Café ££ Offers seafood, pasta, organically grown and local ingredients – and lots of vegetarian options. ⓐ 5-5075 Kuhio Hwy, Suite A ⓣ 826 1191 ⓛ 06.00–21.00 daily

AFTER DARK

Restaurants
The Living Room £££ There are stunning views from this location, which serves up sushi, drinks and live entertainment. At the Princeville Resort. ⓐ 5520 Ka Haku Rd ⓣ 826 9644 ⓦ www.princevillehotelhawaii.com ⓛ 17.30–22.30 daily

Princeville Restaurant and Bar £££ Overlooking the Princeville Golf Course. Cold beer, fresh smoothies, sushi nights on Mondays. ⓐ 5-39.00 Kuhio Hwy ⓣ 826 5050 ⓦ www.princevillehotelhawaii.com ⓛ 07.00–19.00 daily, 17.30–21.00 Mon night sushi

Sabella's at Princeville £££ Italian meets Hawaiian with live entertainment. ⓐ 5300 Ka Haku Rd ⓣ 826 6225 ⓛ 17.30–22.30 Tues–Sun

While the resort offers everything you need – a range of dining options, attractive bars and high-quality restaurants – in order to experience some variety and local flair, head up the road to Hanalei. It's just a few miles from the entrance to the resort.

Bars & clubs
Happy Talk Lounge at Hanalei Bay Resort £ There's jazz and nostalgic music on Saturday nights, and on Sunday a 'Jazz Jam'. On Tuesdays there's a *hula* show at 19.00. ⓐ 5380 Honoiki St ⓣ 826 6522 ⓛ 18.30–21.30 Mon–Sat, 16.00–19.00 Sun

Sushi & Blues in Ching Young Village £ Live reggae, rhythm and blues, rock, local music, dancing and partying. Call to find out what's on. ⓐ 5-5190 Kuhio Hwy ⓣ 826 9701 ⓦ www.sushiandblues.com ⓛ 17.30–02.00 daily

Tahiti Nui £ Friendly local restaurant and bar. It's actually the oldest bar in Hawaii. ⓐ 5-5134 Kuhio Hwy ⓣ 826 6277 ⓦ www.thenui.com ⓛ 14.00–02.00 daily

Lu`aus
Pa`ina o Hanalei at Princeville Resort ££ On the shores of Hanalei Bay. Ceremonial presentation of the classic Kailua pig. ⓐ 5520 Ka Haku Rd ⓣ 826 9644 ⓐ 18.00–20.45 Mon & Thur

The Na Pali Coast

See it from the air in a flight-seeing tour, from the sea on the deck of a yacht, or walk the trail from Haena State Park. The difficulty of getting in and out of the steep, green, cathedral cliffs of the Na Pali Coast has helped keep the landscape unspoiled, uncrowded and spectacular.

Walkers should wear good shoes and bring water, food, insect repellent and sunscreen, and stay on the trail. It's slippery in many places – a walking stick is useful. You'll need a permit if you're planning to camp. Call the park office to find out about permits (**Lihu`e State Park Office** ⓣ 274 3444).

Reservations are required for flight or boat tours. Most boat tours leave from the Port Allen harbour on the south side of the island; flights leave from a variety of locations. Tidal conditions occasionally make it impossible to sail to the Na Pali Coast – ask your tour operator what happens if access isn't possible. Seas can be rough: take precautions if you get seasick.

The unspoiled Na Pali coastline of north Kauai

The Coconut Coast: Kapa`a & Wailua

Kapa`a

Kapa`a is a lively little place that lines both sides of the main highway. There are lots of hotels near Kapa`a, and several good beaches, but heavy traffic dulls the charm. The town is still worth a visit. The old town has a funky, artsy appeal. There's good food to be had, and Kapa`a has a nightlife scene, too. At the northern end of town, there's an open-air market where you can get local produce and handicrafts.

Wailua

The town of Wailua isn't much more than a crossroads where the Wailua River runs into the ocean, but it's the starting point for a number of river-based activities and the turn-off to a few of Kauai's inland natural wonders.

Take a tour up the river to **Fern Grotto**, a lava rock grotto draped in tropical foliage, on Hawaii's only navigable river. The grotto is a natural amphitheatre and you'll almost always find musicians there serenading visitors with traditional songs about Hawaii's natural beauty. If the skies are clear, you'll see the peak of Mount Wai`ale`ale in the distance.

If you'd rather paddle, rent a kayak for a self-guided adventure – or join a tour. Tours provide dry bags, guide service, or shuttle service from a central meeting point to the put-in. Some include lunches, snacks or drinks. The river is fairly protected and smooth and the boats are stable.

TAKING A BREAK

Beezer's Ice Cream £ Burgers and fries, milkshakes, ice cream – exactly what you'd expect from this 1950s-style diner. ⓐ 1380 Kuhio Hwy, #103A ⓣ 822 4411 ⓛ 11.00–22.00 daily

Java Kai £ Quality coffee and baked goods made in house. Friendly and comfortable. ⓐ 4-1384 Kuhio Hwy ⓣ 823 6887 ⓛ 06.00–17.00 daily

Lotus Root Juice Bar and Bakery £ Strictly organic fresh treats, coffee and smoothies for those serious about their ingredients. ⓐ 4-1384 Kuhio Hwy ⓣ 823 6658 ⓦ www.blossominglotus.com ⓛ 07.00–18.00 daily

AFTER DARK

Restaurants
Blossoming Lotus ££ Vegetarian food for people who say they don't like vegetarian food. ⓐ 4504 Kukui St ⓣ 822 7678 ⓦ www.blossominglotus.com ⓛ 11.00–15.00 & 18.00–21.30 daily

House of Noodles ££ Head here for Asian-style noodles – Thai, Vietnamese, Chinese: there's a stunning variety. ⓐ 4-1130 Kuhio Hwy ⓣ 822 2708 ⓛ 10.00–20.00 daily

Kountry Kitchen ££ Serves up pancakes, sandwiches, DIY omelettes and American-style breakfasts. ⓐ 1485 Kuhio Hwy ⓣ 822 3511 ⓛ 06.00–13.30 daily

Mermaid's Café ££ Light meals, bistro-style food, all prepared using fresh ingredients. ⓐ 1384 Kuhio Hwy ⓣ 821 2026 ⓛ 11.00–21.00 daily

Olympic Café ££ This place is always hopping. Grab a balcony seat overlooking Kapa`a's main street. ⓐ 4-1387 Kuhio Hwy ⓣ 822 5825 ⓛ 07.00–21.00 Sun–Thur, 07.00–22.00 Fri & Sat

Scotty's Beachside BBQ ££ Mesquite and hickory smoked meats, homemade BBQ sauce, calorie-laden desserts. ⓐ 4-1546 Kuhio Hwy ⓣ 823 8480 ⓦ www.scottysbbq.com ⓛ 11.00–21.00 daily

Bar
Kauai Tradewinds ££ Offers darts, karaoke, live music, sports on the big-screen TVs and a lively happy hour. ⓐ 484 Kuhio Hwy ⓣ 822 1621 ⓦ www.tradewinds-kauai.com ⓛ 10.00–02.00 daily

Waimea Canyon

When you stand on the edge of this canyon looking out over the water-carved red rock, it's hard to remember that you're in Hawaii, not the American south-west. Waimea Canyon is often compared with Arizona's Grand Canyon, even though it's much smaller at 16 km (10 miles) long and 9,000 m (29,528 ft) deep.

There are no fuel stations on the roads to the canyon, so make sure you fill up before you start. It's cool and often windy at the lookouts. If you're planning to walk in the canyon, bring sturdy shoes, water and food.

There are few facilities once you head inland towards the canyon, but most of the viewpoints have public conveniences. Occasionally, you'll find vendors selling produce and drinks at the viewpoints – but, other than that, shopping is limited to the rather expensive shop at the visitor's centre in Koke`e State Park.

Stop at the lookouts along Waimea Canyon Drive – they're all different, offering views down the canyon, towards the ocean, towards the island of Ni`ihau, and, at the end of the road, views of the Na Pali Coast. You'll see helicopters below you dipping in and out of the canyon walls – it's worth considering taking a flight-seeing trip: it provides a whole new point of view on the geologic beauty.

Polihale State Park

First things first: the road out to the park, while not very long, is a rough stretch. Be aware that this trip may void your rental car contract and, if you break down, it will be expensive to get help. If you do make the drive, take it slowly, let the locals pass, and don't be tempted to drive on to the sand. Park the car on what passes for a road and walk over the rise to the beach.

Once you've tackled the obstacles, you'll find an unspoiled 11-km (6¾-mile) stretch of sand – the longest beach in the Hawaiian Islands. It's perfect for kite flying, sunbathing and long walks. It's not a great swimming beach, though: there are no lifeguards and the spot is known

◆ *Almost as grand...Waimea Canyon*

for rip tides. Bring water, food and sunscreen. Even with the warnings, Polihale is a spectacular stretch of seashore. The west end of the Na Pali cliffs start here, the sunsets are breathtaking, and the crowds are elsewhere.

West Maui

Each winter, thousands of humpback whales frolic in the waters off Maui. The town of **Lahaina** marks the south end of West Maui's resort areas. Lahaina is a historic town that was once the home to Hawaii's high chiefs, the first capital of Hawaii, and a popular port for traders and whalers. Lahaina, Ka`anapali, Napili and Kapalua are all resort towns with hotels, apartments and services that cater to the holidaymakers that come to spend time on West Maui's beaches. Lahaina and Napili have smaller beachfront resorts and apartment complexes; Ka`anapali and Kapalua are home to bigger developments with more elaborate facilities, newer shopping malls and golf courses. All the West Maui accommodations have good access to beaches and are an easy drive to Lahaina's shopping, restaurants and harbour – the departure point for many of the boats that take visitors fishing, whale watching, snorkelling and cruising.

BEACHES

DT Fleming Beach Park
For body and board surfing and swimming. There are picnic tables, public toilets and lifeguards on duty.

Ka`anapali Beach
Located at Ka`anapali Resort, this offers broad white sand, watercraft rentals, surf and windsurfing lessons. There's easy access from all Ka`anapali hotels.

Kapalua Beach
Situated at Kapalua Resort, this is a beautiful beach that offers swimming, snorkelling and diving.

Launiupoko Beach Park
South of Lahaina. A local favourite for the natural pool and lava rock wall. Excellent for children; it has picnic tables and public conveniences.

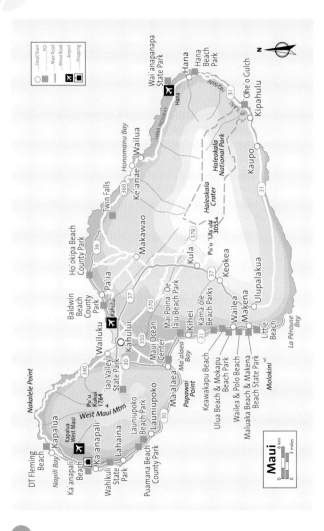

◬ *Escape the crowds in magic Maui*

Napili Bay
South of Kapalua. Offers sandy beaches off which to practise your swimming and snorkelling.

Puamana Beach County Park
Located in Lahaina. Swimming, picnic tables, public toilets, grills for barbecuing and a grassy park. Good for beginner as well as for intermediate surfers.

Wahikuli State Park
In Lahaina. Good for swimming, snorkelling and body boarding. There are public toilets, picnic tables and grills for barbecuing here.

THINGS TO SEE & DO

Maui Ocean Center

Maui Ocean Center at Ma`alaea Harbor has beautiful tanks of tropical fish, a sea turtle viewing area, an enormous tank for watching rays and sharks, tide pools that encourage you to touch the creatures – gently – and lots of educational opportunities. The centre also has quite a good restaurant that serves sustainable seafood options.

ⓐ 192 Ma'alaea Rd, Wailuku ⓣ 270 7000 Ⓦ www.mauioceancenter.com
ⓛ 09.00–17.00 daily ⓘ Admission charge; family packages available

Walk through Lahaina's history

A banyan tree that covers an entire city block and historical buildings built by native Hawaiians or settlers – Lahaina's history is available to

⬥ View sharks and rays at the Maui Ocean Center

those just strolling the streets of this harbourside town. Misbehaving sailors were jailed at the old prison, the football field was once home to a sacred spirit (one wonders where the spirit lives now) – and the Pioneer Inn, Lahaina's first hotel, is still the scene of after-dark drinking and partying. Stop in at the visitor's centre and ask for a walking tour map of the city's 31 sites.

ⓐ 648 Wharf St ⓣ 310 1117 ⓦ www.visitlahaina.com ⓒ Daily

TAKING A BREAK

BJ's Chicago Pizzeria £ Deep-pan pizza, pasta, salads and sandwiches are on offer here. Great for lunch or dinner. ⓐ 730 Front St ⓣ 661 0700 ⓦ www.bjsrestaurants.com ⓒ 11.00–23.00 daily

Livewire Internet Café £ Coffee, bagels, baked goods and other snacks. ⓐ 612 Front St ⓣ 661 4213 ⓒ 06.00–21.00 daily

Maui Grown Coffee £ Sample the varieties of coffee grown on this plantation. ⓐ 277 Lahainaluna Rd ⓣ 661 2728 ⓦ www.mauigrowncoffee.com ⓒ 06.30–17.00 Mon–Sat

AFTER DARK

Restaurants
Bamboo Bar & Grill ££ Casual and affordable Thai and Vietnamese food. ⓐ 505 Front St ⓣ 667 4051 ⓒ 11.00–14.00 & 17.00–23.30 Wed–Sat

Cheeseburger in Paradise ££ Local hangout serving big burgers. There's some live music and a lively bar. ⓐ 811 Front St ⓣ 661 4855 ⓦ www.cheeseburgerland/users/lahainadetails.aspx ⓒ 08.00–22.00 daily

Lahaina Grill ££ Repeatedly voted the best restaurant on Maui. Dishes use local ingredients and fresh seafood. ⓐ 127 Lahainaluna Rd ⓣ 667 5117 ⓦ www.lahainagrill.com ⓒ 18.00 onwards daily

🔺 *Linger in Lahaina*

Kimo's Restaurant £££ Fine dining with views of the nearby islands. Seafood and steaks and a popular bar upstairs. 📍 845 Front St, #A 📞 661 4811 🌐 www.kimosmaui.com 🕐 11.30–15.00 & 17.00–22.30 daily

Clubs
Hula Grill ££ Lively bar in a beach-hut style, lots of *hula* kitsch. On the beach in Whaler's Village. 📍 2435 Kaanapali Pkwy 📞 667 6636 🌐 www.hulagrill.com 🕐 17.00–21.30 daily

Moose McGillycuddy's ££ Drinks and a big dance floor – you'll hear it before you see it. Look up, it's on the second floor. 📍 844 Front St 📞 667 7758 🌐 www.mooserestaurantgroup.com 🕐 07.30–22.00 daily

Paradise Bluz ££ Jazz, live music, dancing and comedy. Dress code and cover charge. 📍 744 Front St 📞 667 5299 🕐 21.00–02.00 daily

Warren and Annabelle's ££ Appetisers, a bar, fancy desserts and a magic show. 📍 900 Front St 📞 667 6244 🌐 www.warrenandannabelles.com 🕐 17.00–23.30 Mon–Sat ❗ Must be aged 21 or over

Lu`aus
Drums of the Pacific at the Hyatt Regency at Ka`anapali Beach £££ Take an imaginary journey through the islands of Polynesia. Admission price includes an all-you-can-eat buffet and cocktails. 📍 200 Nohea Kai Drive 📞 667 4727 🌐 www.maui-hyatt.com 🕐 17.00–20.00 daily

The Feast at Lele £££ In downtown Lahaina. Dinner show with Polynesian dancers and a *lu`au* buffet. 📍 505 Front St 📞 667 5353 🌐 www.feastatlele.com 🕐 18.00–21.00 daily

Old Lahaina *Lu`au* £££ The history of the Polynesian migration opens the show. 📍 1251 Front St 📞 667 1998 🌐 www.oldlahainaluau.com 🕐 18.00–21.00 daily

Kihei

Kihei's location on Maui's sunny south shore makes it a perfect sun lover's retreat. There's an endless selection of apartments, hotels and holiday homes – interspersed with shops. While there's not much charm in the architecture, the beaches are soft golden sand, there's good snorkelling within walking distance of most hotels and there are plenty of after-dark diversions. It's a busy beach town that's a little more affordable than West Maui and Lahaina – though travellers seeking luxury will find it further south towards Wailea and Makena.

BEACHES

Kama`ole Beach Parks I, II and III
This series of beaches along the strip in Kihei has great swimming and snorkelling, access to shopping and plenty of facilities. Close to Kihei resorts. Lifeguards, volleyball court, public toilets and showers.

Keawakapu Beach
Beautiful views, nice for beach walks. Half a mile from Wailea Resort.

Kihei Beach
A series of beaches, coves and tide pools along the Kihei coastline. There are lifeguards, public toilets and picnic facilities.

Mai Poina `Oe Ia`u Beach Park
Good for swimming, kite-surfing and windsurfing. Facilities include picnic tables, showers and public conveniences. In winter you can enjoy whale watching from the beach.

Makena Beach State Park
Two beaches – Big Beach, a broad stretch of sand, and Little Beach (clothing optional) with body surfing. There are picnic tables and public toilets here.

Maluaka Beach

Next to the Maui Prince Hotel, this provides excellent swimming and snorkelling. A good place for spotting sea turtles.

Mokapu Beach Park

Swimming and snorkelling. Equipment is available for rent on stalls in front of the Renaissance Wailea Beach Resort.

Polo Beach

Swimming and snorkelling. There are picnic tables and public toilets.

Ulua Beach

Great for swimming, snorkelling and beachcombing.

⬤ *Excellent swimming and snorkelling are on offer at Kihei*

Wailea Beach

There's good swimming and a paved beach walk here, as well as public conveniences and equipment rentals.

TAKING A BREAK

Alexander's Fish, Chicken & Ribs £ Combo plates of fish, chicken, shrimp, ribs or veggies. Counter service. Across the street from Kalama Park.
🅰 1913 S Kihei Rd ☎ 874 0788 🕐 11.00–21.00 daily

Kihei Caffe £ Nice outdoor dining area, burgers, salads – and for tardy risers, breakfast is served until 14.00. 🅰 1945 S Kihei Rd ☎ 879 2230
🕐 05.00–14.00 daily

Maui Tacos £ Cheap, fast, fresh and delicious Mexican food. Expect a wait. 🅰 2411 S Kihei Rd ☎ 879 5005 🆆 www.mauitacos.com/hi.htm
🕐 09.00–21.00 daily

Café O'Lei Kihei ££ Local seafood, steaks and sushi, plus a great dessert menu. Dinner reservations. Upstairs at the Rainbow Mall.
🅰 2439 S Kihei Rd ☎ 891 1368 🆆 www.cafeoleirestaurants.com
🕐 10.30–22.30 Tues–Sun

Hirohachi ££ Traditional Japanese food of the best quality. 🅰 1881 S Kihei Rd ☎ 875 7474 🕐 17.00–21.30 Tues, Sat & Sun, 11.30–14.30 & 17.30–21.30 Wed–Fri

Mulligan's on the Blue ££ British food – fish and chips, shepherd's pie – served in an Irish pub. There is occasional live Irish or local music.
🅰 Wailea Blue Golf Course, 100 Kaukahi St ☎ 874 1131
🆆 www.mulligansontheblue.com 🕐 08.00–01.00 daily

Pupu Lounge Seafood & Grill ££ Big appetiser plates, cocktails and full meals. 🅰 1945 S Kihei Rd ☎ 875 4111 🕐 12.00–22.00 daily

Humuhumunukunukuapua`a £££ Fine dining and a huge fish tank. Pick your own lobster. ⓐ Grand Wailea Resort, 3850 Wailea Alanui Drive ❶ 875 1234 ⓦ www.grandwailea.com/dining/humu.asp ❺ 17.00–21.00 daily ❶ Reservations recommended

AFTER DARK

Kahale's Beach Club ££ A local hangout right in the middle of the tourist village. Serves bar snacks and drinks. ⓐ 36 Kealea Place ❶ 875 7711 ❺ 10.00–02.00 daily

Lotus Lounge ££ After 22.00, the Fire Dragon Bistro transforms into a late-night dance club. ⓐ 3750 Wailea Alanui ❶ 879 6088 ❺ 22.00–01.30 Fri & Sat

South Shore Tiki Lounge ££ Reggae music, Hawaiian food, tropical drinks and a great island vibe. ⓐ 1913 S Kihei Rd ❶ 874 6444 ⓦ www.southshoretikilounge.com ❺ 11.00–24.00 daily

Lu`aus
Honua`ula, Return to Sacred Lands at the Wailea Beach Marriott ££
Legends of fire goddesses, mermaids and Maui. ⓐ 3700 Wailea Alanui Drive ❶ 875 7710 ❺ 17.00–20.00 Mon, Thur, Fri & Sat

**Sunset *Lu`au* at the Maui Prince Hotel ££** A *lu`au* in a secluded, romantic setting. ⓐ 5400 Makena Alanui ❶ 877 4852 ⓦ www.princeresortsHawaii.com/maui-luau.php ❺ 17.30–20.30 Tues & Thur

Maui excursions

THE `IAO VALLEY & WAILUKU

The `Iao stream has sliced a lush green valley through the volcanic rock, leaving the **`Iao Needle**, a 689-m (2,260-ft) monumental stone peak. A short walk through `Iao Valley State Park ends at a viewpoint at the base of the needle. The park contains native plants, taro patches and native Hawaiian structures. This peaceful site, covered in lush tropical foliage with the `Iao stream burbling quietly below, was once the site of a bloody battle between Maui's soldiers and Kamehameha I's army. **Wailuku**, which is the county seat of Maui, gets overlooked by visitors blowing through on their way up to the `Iao Needle, but it's worth a stop. Main Street has several antique and second-hand stores where you'll find Chinese furniture, Japanese kimonos and other vintage Asian treasures. It's also got a surprising selection of excellent restaurants.

TAKING A BREAK

Maui Bake Shop and Deli £ The French-trained baker produces European-style breads as well as deli items – sandwiches, salads, quiches – and desserts. ❷ 2092 Vineyard St ❶ 242 0064 ❸ 06.00–15.00 Mon–Fri, 07.00–13.00 Sat

Café Marc Aurel ££ Bistro food, an outdoor patio, and an amazing variety of wines by the glass. ❷ 28 N Market St ❶ 244 0852 ❾ www.cafemarcaurel.com ❸ 07.00–21.00 Mon–Sat

Saigon Café ££ It's easy to miss the entrance, but don't give up looking, you'll find some of the best Vietnamese food in the islands here. ❷ 1792 Main St ❶ 243 9560 ❸ 10.00–21.30 Mon–Sat, 10.00–20.30 Sun

Sam Sato's ££ Maui-style noodle dishes with grilled meat. Dip the noodles in the bowl of broth on the side. ❷ 1750 Wili Pa Loop ❶ 244 7124 ❸ 07.00–14.00 daily

🔺 *Lush foliage and volcanic rock in `Iao Valley*

HANA

Before you head to Hana, you'll get a fair idea of the epic nature of the trip from the 'I survived the road to Hana' t-shirts on sale in the souvenir shops. If you drive carefully and courteously round the 600 curves, and have a full tank of fuel, it's not exactly an ordeal. Stop in at Pa`ia to fill up on petrol and snacks – it's your last chance for petrol before Hana. Pick up a guide to the road, too: there are worthwhile sights on the way, but almost no signs indicating them.

BEACHES

Hana Beach Park

Good swimming: this beach is popular with local families.

Wai`anapanapa State Park

There's camping and cabins overlooking the black-sand beach here. Good swimming, snorkelling and freshwater pools in caves.

THINGS TO SEE & DO

Most visitors take one day to drive to Hana and back from their Kihei or West Maui hotels. That's a shame. Day trippers miss out on the local feel of Hana after dark, on the pleasure of seeing the sights with almost no visitors, and the ease of taking this long drive at a leisurely pace. Stay overnight in Hana if you can. There are a handful of smaller hotels and B&Bs, as well as the **Hana Maui Hotel** (📞 321 4262) in the centre of Hana. Be warned, though, that while there are places to stay, there aren't many of them and most close early. Pick up supplies at the **Hasegawa General Store**, Hana's shopping institution, but do so before they close at 19.00 – earlier on Sundays.

`Ohe`o Gulch

The culmination of most trips to Hana is `Ohe`o Gulch, a natural playground with pools for swimming, walking trails, a bamboo forest,

⬥ *The rocky coast road to Hana*

waterfalls and historic sites. There are public toilets and a visitor's centre near the car park. `Ohe`o Gulch – 16 km (10 miles) past Hana – is in the Kipahulu division of Haleakala National Park. An admission fee covers entrance to this and Haleakala Crater if your visits are carried out within three days of each other

TAKING A BREAK

Hana Ranch Restaurant ££ Casual dining and a takeaway window. This restaurant serves Polynesian-inspired ranch food and is located in Hana town centre. ⓐ Hana Hwy ⓣ 248 8255 ⓦ www.hotelhanamaui.com ⓛ 18.00–20.30 Wed, Fri & Sat

Paniolo Lounge ££ Set on the hotel verandah, this serves lighter meals, espresso and cocktails. There's also live music by local musicians.
ⓐ Hana Hwy ❶ 321 4262 ⓦ www.hotelhanamaui.com
❶ 11.30–22.00 daily

Ka'uiki £££ Also at the Hana Maui Hotel, this features Pacific Island and regional cuisine including local fresh fish. ⓐ Hana Hwy ❶ 321 4262
ⓦ www.hotelhanamaui.com ❶ 09.00–22.00 daily ❶ Dress code for dinner and reservations recommended

UPCOUNTRY

The term 'upcountry' refers to the lower slopes of **Haleakala** and includes the villages of **Pa`ia** (where the road to Hana starts), **Kula**, **Makawao** and **Ulupalakua**. Upcountry offers horse-riding and biking opportunities – biking down the volcano is a popular one – and lots of good places to eat. Pa`ia is an attractive town with shopping, galleries, a Hindu temple and windy beaches – the last making it a popular spot for windsurfers and kite boarders. Makawao retains its cowboy feel – there's a terrific Western Wear store – even while transforming itself into a gallery browser's dream. Kula has agritourism sites – visit the **Kula Lavender Farm**, **Tedeschi Vineyards** and **Surfing Goat Dairy**.

TAKING A BREAK

Café des Amis ££ Crêpes, seafood, salads, espresso and smoothies.
ⓐ 42 Baldwin Ave ❶ 579 6323 ❶ 08.30–20.30 daily

Pa`ia Fish Market ££ Casual, not quite fast-food-style restaurant. Specialises in fresh seafood. ⓐ 100 Hana Hwy ❶ 579 8030
❶ 11.00–21.30 daily

La Provence ££ French bistro-style lunches and dinners, pastries, salads and sandwiches. ⓐ 3158 Lower Kula Rd ❶ 878 1313
ⓦ www.laprovencekula.com ❶ 07.00–21.00 Wed–Sun

Ulupalakua Ranch Store ££ This is a meat-eater's paradise.
Your sandwich originally grazed here too. ⓐ HC 1 Box 901 Kula
ⓣ 878 2561 ⓦ www.ulupalakuaranch.com ⓛ 09.30–17.00 daily

AFTER DARK

Restaurants
Jacques Northshore Bar and Grill ££ Sushi, seafood, salads, outdoor
dining. ⓐ 120 Hana Hwy ⓣ 579 8844 ⓛ 11.30–15.00 & 17.00–22.00 daily
ⓘ Reservations recommended

Makawao Steak House £££ Head here for steaks, seafood, pork, poultry
and big lunch plates. ⓐ 3612 Baldwin Ave ⓣ 572 8711 ⓛ 17.30–21.30 daily

Mama's Fish House £££ Situated on the beach just north of Pa`ia, this
local favourite dishes up excellent seafood within a beach-hut ambience.
ⓐ 799 Poho Place ⓣ 579 8488 ⓦ www.mamasfishhouse.com
ⓛ 11.00–14.00 & 16.30–21.30 daily ⓘ Reservations recommended

Bars & clubs
Casanova £ Dancing, cocktails, ladies' nights and live entertainment.
ⓐ 1188 Makawao Ave ⓣ 572 0220 ⓦ www.casanovamaui.com
ⓛ 11.30–14.00 & 17.30–21.30 Mon–Sat

Charley's £ Local bands, live music – rock, blues, reggae, country and DJ
nights. ⓐ 142 Hana Hwy ⓣ 579 9453 ⓛ 07.00–22.00 daily

Stopwatch Sports Bar and Grill £ Big screens for watching the game,
beer and bar food, some live music. ⓐ 1127 Makawao Ave ⓣ 572 1380
ⓛ 11.00–02.00 daily

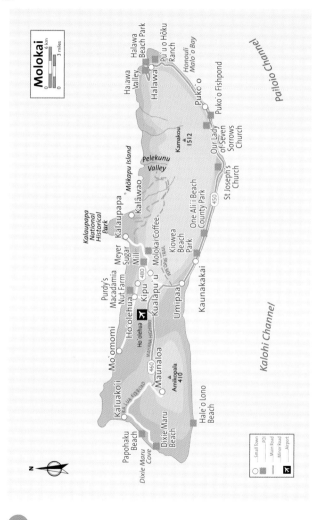

Molokai

0 ___ 6 km
0 ___ 3 miles

Pailoio Channel

Halawa Beach Park

Pu'u o Hōku Ranch

Ha'awa Valley

Halawa

Honouli Malo'o Bay

Puko'o

Puko'o Fishpond

Kamakou ▲ 1512

Our Lady of Seven Sorrows Church

Pelekunu Valley

Mōkapu Island

Kalaupapa National Historical Park

Kalaupapa

Kalāwao

St Joseph's Church

450

Meyer Sugar Mill

Molokai Coffee

One Ali'i Beach County Park

PEPE'OPAE TRAIL

Purdy's Macadamia Nut Farm

480

Kipu

Kualapu'u

Kiowea Beach Park

Kaunakakai

Ho'olehua

Ho'olehua

Mo'omomi

Umipaa

Kaloha'o Road

MAHANA HIGHWAY

Kalaupapa

Maunaloa

Amikopala 410

Kaluako'i

Kalohi Channel

Papohaku Beach

Dixie Maru Cove

Dixie Maru Beach

Hale'o Lono Beach

460

N

○ Small Town
■ POI
— Main Road
— Minor Road
✈ Airport

Molokai

Nothing taller than a coconut tree: that's the zoning law on Molokai. This approach has slowed development, making Molokai a smaller, quieter version of Hawai`i – in fact, reminiscent of a Hawai`i in earlier times. There aren't many tourist facilities on the 'Most Hawaiian' island, but there are plenty of things to recommend Molokai. The beaches are uncrowded, there's very little traffic, and the locals still make time to chat with visitors. Molokai is a great 'get away from it all' destination.

BEACHES

The beaches on Molokai don't offer much by way of services, they're not close to shopping and you're lucky if you find one with public toilets or running water. But they are clean and uncrowded; often you'll be the only visitor there.

Dixie Maru Cove
Popular with families: there's good snorkelling here when the surf is down. It's located at the end of Kaluakoi Road on the west side of the island.

Halawa Beach Park
Lies at the east end of the road in Halawa. It's a rocky grey-sand beach with views of the cliffs. There is a small picnic shelter and public conveniences at the entrance to the park.

Hale`o Lono Beach
A good place for whale watching in season. There are no facilities. Public access is via a dirt road owned by the Molokai Ranch. Follow Mokio Street, just before the post office in Maunaloa, to the end.

Honouli Malo`o Bay
A very pretty cove with good surfing and snorkelling. No facilities. Just after Mile Marker 21 on the road to Halawa.

Kiowea Beach Park

This attractive picnic spot is under renovation – the coconut groves are being replanted and the beach is being cleaned up. Not good for swimming, but it's a lovely sunset picnic stop. On Highway 460, west of Kaunakakai.

One Ali`i Beach County Park

This is one of the few beaches with facilities, but unfortunately it's not a good swimming beach because of the shallow, murky waters – it's on the site of a former fishpond. Just west of Kaunakakai on Highway 460.

THINGS TO SEE & DO

Agritourism

Molokai has a handful of local agritourism sights that you can enjoy without the crowds you get on the larger islands. **Molokai Coffee** at Kualapu`u offers horse-drawn carriage tours through their coffee plantation – or you can simply stop in at the visitor's centre to taste the coffee.

At **Purdy's Macadamia Nut Farm**, the enthusiastic owner will share history, the health benefits of the macadamia nut, and samples of macadamia nut products – which you can buy from his unassuming shed. The once profitable **Meyer Sugar Mill** has been restored and has a small collection of Hawaiian artefacts and changing cultural exhibits.

Molokai excursions

HALAWA VALLEY

The road to Halawa Valley winds past empty beaches, through tiny villages, around sharp turns with beautiful lookouts, and culminates at the grey sand of Halawa Beach Park. Halawa is a traditional Hawaiian village where the lifestyle of old Hawaii is in revival. Taro patches and fishponds are being restored and stories of Hawaiian ancestors are retold.

Guided hikes and cultural tours of the valley's sacred sites are a good way to learn about the island's history and how the community is working to revive Hawaiian values. Most of the land here is privately owned and solo exploration is discouraged – book your guided adventure before you head into the valley or end your independent adventure at the spectacular beach.

KALAUPAPA

In 1873 Father Damien arrived in Kalaupapa – a near inaccessible settlement – to minister to a community of native Hawaiians who had been cast out from their homes. These victims of Hansen's disease – then called leprosy – lived in poverty and isolation at a spur of land on Molokai's coast. Father Damien spent his life working to improve the lot of these neglected people. The settlement remains an isolated place, reached by a steep 3.2-km (2-mile) track on the bluff above.

Kalaupapa is a national park dedicated to educating visitors about the disease. The community is also a place where current residents and sufferers of Hansen's disease may live out their lives in comfort.

Visitors can take a guided tour, riding a mule down a track. Walkers who don't want to make the uphill climb all the way back can arrange to fly out in a helicopter – or fly both ways. Note that there are strict rules around visiting the community – permits are required and no children under the age of 16 are allowed. Guests must bring their own supplies as there are no services in the community. Contact the National Park Service or the Molokai Visitor's Association for help in planning your visit.

Kalaupapa National Historical Park ❶ 567 6802
Molokai Visitor's Association ❶ 553 3876

KAUNAKAKAI

This ramshackle town is the heart of Molokai. It's home to the very popular **Kanemitsu Bakery**, where locals line up in the middle of the night to get their hot, sweet Molokai bread. Molokai's shopping is based here – if you need groceries, a cash machine, souvenirs, a cup of coffee, internet access, eggs and rice, or a snorkel mask, this is the place to come.

TAKING A BREAK

Cafés, restaurants & bars

Visitors don't come to Molokai seeking nightlife or gourmet meals, but there are a few places where you can get good island-style food or catch live music by local bands.

⬤ *Halawa Valley: empty beaches and fine views*

Kanemitsu's Bakery £ The interior isn't attractive, but the service is friendly and the food is fresh. Closes early, breakfast and lunch only. Go at dawn if you want a decent selection of hot bread, or ask the locals about the late-night bread run. ⓐ 79 Ala Malama St ⓣ 553 5855 ⓛ Bakery 05.30–18.30; restaurant Wed–Mon 05.30–11.30

Manae Goods & Grindz £ A general store with a breakfast and lunch counter. The last stop for food if you're heading to the east end of the island. ⓐ Kamehameha Hwy ⓣ 558 8498 ⓛ 08.00–18.00 daily

Stanley's Coffee House £ Island-style breakfasts, *saimin*, eggs and rice, baked goods – and the best coffee in town. ⓐ 125 Puali St, Kaunakakai ⓣ 553 9966 ⓛ 06.30–16.00 Mon–Sat

Hotel Molokai ££ Live music on the weekends and a full bar. A local hangout at this remodelled hotel on the beach just east of Kaunakakai. ⓐ Kamehameha V Hwy ⓣ 535 5347 ⓦ www.hotelmolokai.com ⓛ 07.00–14.00 & 18.00–21.00 Sat–Thur, 07.00–14.00 & 16.00–21.00 Fri ⓘ Dinner reservations recommended

Kualapuu Cookhouse ££ Don't be fooled by the burger bar/roadside diner look of the exterior. This offers big helpings, fresh food and reasonable prices. Another popular local hangout. ⓐ Farrington Hwy ⓣ 567 9655 ⓛ 07.00–14.00 Mon, 07.00–20.00 Tues–Sat

Maunaloa Dining Room £££ At Molokai Ranch. Fine dining, steaks, seafood – and views of the sun setting from the dining room. For lighter meals and cocktails on the *lana`i* (verandah), try the bar. ⓐ 100 Maunaloa Hwy ⓣ 660 2824 ⓛ 07.00–10.30 & 18.00–21.00 daily ⓘ Reservations recommended for dinner

◐ *Enjoy the sandy beaches of Lana`i*

Lana`i

Pineapples once covered the red earth landscape of this privately owned island where tourism is gaining ground. The village is still home to families who remember picking the fruits. Lana`i is popular with luxury travellers and golfers who want to play the island's scenic and exclusive course. A few day trippers come by ferry from Maui to take the 4WD roads to Lana`i's nearly empty beaches.

A warning to ferry passengers – the morning crossing from Maui is quite pleasant, but the afternoon return can turn into 'the washing machine' – a rough swell that can send the sturdiest of sailors running for the rail. If you get seasick, take precautions.

BEACHES

Hulupo`e Beach Park

There are natural pools here, along with snorkelling, rock pooling and a wide sandy beach. The beach provides the best swimming on the island and it is very popular with the locals. There are public toilets and showers, picnic tables and plenty of parking.

Polihua Beach

Accessible by 4WD only, this has great views of Molokai. Beautiful white sand, no facilities.

Shipwreck Beach

Accessible by 4WD only, Shipwreck Beach is the site of many shipwrecks caused by the strong currents and shallow reefs. On the plus side there are great views, good walking, petroglyphs, lighthouse ruins and the chance to do some beachcombing. The downside is that there are dangerous tides and no facilities.

TAKING A BREAK

Blue Ginger Café £ Sandwiches and local food, homemade bread. Popular with locals. ❷ 407 Seventh St ☎ 565 6363 🕔 06.00–20.00 daily

Canoe's £ Local food – eggs and rice, *saimin*, sandwiches, burgers and Spam *musubi*. ❷ 419 Seventh St ☎ 565 6537 🕔 06.30–13.00 Thur–Tues

Pele's Other Garden Deli ££ Casual Italian food, pizza, sandwiches for lunch, plus a bar. ❷ 811 Houston St ☎ 565 9628
ⓦ www.pelesothergarden.com 🕔 10.00–14.00 & 17.00–20.00 Mon–Fri

The Experience at Koele Clubhouse £££ Casual dining overlooking the first hole of the golf course. Light meals, breakfast and lunch only. ❷ One Keomoku Hwy ☎ 565 4563
ⓦ www.fourseasons.com/koele/dining/the_experience_at_koele_clubhouse.html 🕔 10.30–16.30 daily

The Formal Dining Room at Koele Lodge £££ Grand dining using local ingredients when possible. ❷ One Keomoku Hwy ☎ 565 4580
ⓦ www.fourseasons.com/koele/dining.html 🕔 18.00–21.30 daily
ⓘ Dress code; booking required

Ihilani Restaurant at the Manele Bay Four Seasons £££ A gourmet splurge with stunning views. ❷ One Manele Bay Rd ☎ 565 2296
ⓦ www.fourseasons.com/manelebay/dining/ihilani.html 🕔 18.00–21.30
Tues–Sat ⓘ Dress code; booking required

**Lana`i City Grille £££** Hawaii Regional Cuisine (see page 96) at the plantation-style Hotel Lana`i. Fresh seafood, Hawaiian ingredients, live music on weekends. ❷ 828 Lana`i Ave ☎ 565 7211
ⓦ www.hotellanai.com/grille.html 🕔 17.00–21.00 Wed–Sun
ⓘ Booking recommended

Lana`i excursions

LANA`I CITY

This little planned community was laid out along a grid system, with its name of Lana`i City reflecting the founder's ambitions to develop the place into a grand home for the workers and businessmen behind the plantation. The city is centred around Dole Park, a big playing field and lawn lined with markets, galleries and a few restaurants.

The Lana`i Culture and Heritage Center

The island of Lana`i has 1,000 years of history; only 70 of those years were dominated by pineapple growing. The cultural centre has a small collection of Hawaiian artefacts and teaches visitors about the development of modern day Lana`i.

ⓐ In Lana`i City ☎ 565 7177 Ⓦ www.lanaichc.org ⏰ 09.00–15.00 Mon–Fri
❶ Donations welcomed

🔺 *See red at the Garden of the Gods*

THE GARDEN OF THE GODS & POLIHUA BEACH

You'll need a 4WD vehicle to make the rough trip through the spare and beautiful landscape of the mistranslated Garden of the Gods. The Hawaiian name of this place – Keahiakawelo – means 'Where Kewelo makes fire'. Legend tells of a contest between two priests, one from Molokai, one from Lana`i, over who could keep a fire burning the longer. Kewelo, the Lana`i priest, is said to have used everything in the area to keep his fire alive, explaining the lack of vegetation in the area now. The wind-sculpted landscape is stunning and bare, in red and orange colours more reminiscent of the Australian outback than tropical Hawaii.

Polihua Beach is the swathe of white sand at the end of the road. The surf is rough and it can be very windy, so it's not a sunbathing and swimmer's paradise, but you may very well be the only visitor on the beach. Bring a picnic and find a sheltered spot in trees to take in the sound of the surf.

THE MUNRO TRAIL

Lana`i's other 4WD adventure is a one-lane red earth road that offers sweeping views of neighbouring Maui and Maunalei Gulch, and takes you to the track that heads up to Lana`i's highest point, Sweetheart Rock. **Pu`u Pehe**, the Hawaiian name of Sweetheart Rock, is the site of a tragic Lana`i legend. A princess from Maui was captured by a Lana`i warrior who, mad with jealousy, imprisoned her in a cave near the rock. When the surf turned high, the warrior realised his error and returned to rescue the princess, but he was too late. After burying her in a cave on Sweetheart Rock, he leapt to his own death.

If you arrive at Lana`i by ferry, you'll see Pu`u Pehe as you enter the harbour, but you can also view the rock from a trail that starts in Hulupo`e Beach Park. The cliffs are steep here – stay on the path.

◑ *The Hawaiian and United States' national flags*

Food & drink

Hawaii's history as a tourist destination means that there's no shortage of places to get a meal. Casual attire is acceptable almost everywhere, though an evening out is a good excuse to splash out on some festive *aloha* wear. Some of the more upmarket restaurants may operate a dress code. A 15 per cent tip is customary, though more is always welcome for exceptional service. In Waikiki and Honolulu, trendier restaurants may require you to book – call ahead if you're not sure.

Dinner tends to be served on the early side with kitchens closing around 20.00–21.00. If the sun is going down, it's time to head off to eat dinner!

HAWAII REGIONAL CUISINE (HRC)

Until the early 1980s, Hawaii had an unfortunate reputation for frozen fish and expensive ingredients shipped in from faraway places. The Hawaii Regional Cuisine (HRC) movement changed all that by ensuring that fresh local ingredients were served. HRC combines local produce with the diverse ethnic styles of the islands. Fresh seafood is widely available, but Hawaiian beef is also famous for its quality.

LU`AU FOODS & PLATE LUNCHES

A *lu`au* is a fun way to enjoy traditional food. Roasted *kalua* pig – slow cooked in an underground oven – and *poi* (paste made from taro root) are staples, as are *lomi-lomi* salmon (raw salmon marinated with onions and tomatoes) and *haupia* (coconut custard).

If you want a less formal meal, pick up a 'plate lunch' at a diner or drive-in restaurant. This consists of servings of white rice, macaroni salad and a meat or fish dish, all washed down with fruit punch.

ETHNIC VARIETIES

Hawaii's cultural melting pot means that there's a great variety of ethnic food – some of the best meals at the best prices can be had in the little Thai, Vietnamese and Chinese restaurants that are hidden away in local shopping malls. Excellent sushi is easy to find, as are upmarket places serving Pacific Rim cuisine – a mix of Chinese, Japanese and mainland US flavours (for example) all on the same plate. European food is plentiful as well – Italian, Greek and French are all available.

VEGETARIANS

Hawaii can be challenging for vegetarians, but most restaurants do offer a few vegetarian selections. The Vegetarian Society of Hawaii website (ⓦ www.vsh.org) lists restaurants and markets that offer vegetarian options. Chinese, Thai and Vietnamese restaurants almost always list vegetarian dishes. Strict vegetarians should enquire about ingredients, however, as there's no guarantee that a vegetable dish won't have been cooked in chicken stock, for example.

DRINKS

Beachside hotels and bars offer a seemingly endless variety of tropical cocktails. They can be expensive, but it's an essential island experience to taste the tropics while watching the sun go down. Ask for a 'virgin' version – one with no alcohol – if you don't drink.

Consider a Blue Hawaiian, invented at the Hilton Hawaiian Village Resort in 1957 by bartender Harry Yee – it's rum, vodka, blue Curaçao, pineapple juice and sweet and sour mix. Or a traditional Mai Tai, which is rum, orange Curaçao, orange and lime juice, Orgeat and sugar syrup.

DESSERTS & TREATS

Haupia is a coconut-based pudding – it's common at *lu`aus* or to follow your plate lunch. Shave ice is a giant snow cone covered in sweet flavoured syrup such as mango, guava or passion fruit. Macadamia nut candies are everywhere, or try chocolate-covered Kona coffee beans for an extra boost. Hawai`i has an amazing variety of island-made ice creams, often flavoured with Kona coffee and macadamia nuts or tropical fruit.

Menu decoder

Here are some of the dishes and terms that you might encounter in restaurants and bakeries around the island.

Ahi Tuna

Bento Japanese packed lunch that consists of rice, fish or meat and vegetable side dishes

Haupia A coconut pudding that's the consistency of jelly

Huli-huli Chicken barbecued in a sauce made with brown sugar cane, soy sauce and fresh ginger

Imu An underground oven, a pit lined with stones

Kalua pig A *lu`au* tradition, roasted in an *imu*

Kulolo A dessert made of taro, brown sugar and coconut milk

Lau-lau Pork and butterfish wrapped first in *lu`au* leaves, then ti leaves, then steamed. To eat, you unwrap the bundle and eat the spinach-like filling

Loco moco A breakfast dish consisting of a hamburger with a fried egg on top, served with rice and gravy

Lomi-lomi salmon Cold diced salmon with onions and tomatoes

Malasada A Portuguese doughnut, fried and rolled in sugar

Manapua A type of Chinese dim-sum (dumpling), with cured pork

Opah Moonfish, a dense fish similar to swordfish in texture

Opakapaka Crimson snapper, Hawaiian pink snapper; has white or light pink meat and a delicate flavour

Opihi Limpets

Pipikaula Dried beef, similar to beef jerky but not as dry

Poi A purplish paste made from taro, a staple of the traditional Hawaiian diet

Poke ('po-kay') A *pupu* (appetiser or snack) made

of diced raw fish (often *ahi*) with soy sauce, green onions and fresh herbs

Pupu platter An appetiser plate

Saimin ('sy-min') Soup with noodles and meat or fish, similar to Japanese *ramen*

Spam musubi Japanese-style sushi rice wrapped in seaweed and topped with Spam. Spam is an active participant in Hawaiian cuisine!

⬤ *Fast food Hawaiian-style*

LIFESTYLE

Shopping

SHOPPING MALLS

If shopping is your thing, you'll love Waikiki. The Ala Moana Shopping
Center has four floors of shopping with 260 stores; the Waikiki Beach
Walk offers more upmarket shopping and dining. For an amazing variety
of handicrafts and souvenirs, try the International Marketplace under
the giant banyan trees on Kalakaua Avenue – it's open late and is a lively
browsing destination after dark. The Waikiki Trolley Pink Line is known as
'the shopping line' – buy a trolley pass to shop until you drop!

Ala Moana Center ⓐ 1441 Kapi`olani Blvd, Honolulu
International Marketplace ⓐ 2330 Kalakaua Ave, Honolulu
Wyndham Waikiki Beach Walk ⓐ 227 Lewers St, Honolulu

The King's Shops and the soon-to-be-opened Queen's Shops are just
outside the Waikaloa Hilton on the Big Island; further south you will find
The Shops at Wailea. Whaler's Village is in the heart of the Ka`anapali
resort area on Maui – and there's also the Lahaina Cannery Mall. Kauai
has the Coconut Marketplace between Wailua and Kapa`a.

Coconut Marketplace ⓐ 4-484 Kuhio Hwy, Kauai
King's Shops ⓐ 69-250 Waikoloa Beach Drive #B10, Waikoloa
Lahaina Cannery Mall ⓐ 1221 Honoapiilani Hwy, Lahaina
The Shops at Wailea ⓐ 3750 Wailea Alanui Drive, Kihei
Whaler's Village ⓐ 2435 Ka`anapali Pkwy, Lahaina

FARMER'S MARKETS

Farmer's markets are thriving on the islands. In Kailua-Kona Village on
Hawai`i, you can buy shell jewellery, Kona coffee and wood carvings.
Hilo's farmer's market is becoming a must-visit destination for the take-
away food and the amazing scene.

ALOHA WEAR

For quality *aloha* wear, look for brands by Tommy Bahama, Tori Richards,
Kalakaua or Reyn Spooner. The higher quality shirts have patterns that

match in front and pockets cut so that the pattern isn't broken. Vintage patterns are rare, so snap them up if you find them.

UKULELES

Souvenir ukuleles are everywhere, but if you're shopping for a real instrument, go to a proper music store and expect to spend at least $100. You can visit ukulele workshops to see how a real instrument is made.

Kamaka Ukulele ⓐ 550 South St, Honolulu

**Kanile`a Ukulele** ⓐ 46-216 Kahuhipa St, Kane`ohe

Ko`olau Guitar & Ukulele Co ⓐ 401 N Cane St, #A10, Wahiawa

HANDICRAFTS

If you're looking for genuine Hawaiian-made objects, museum shops in places like Bailey House on Maui or Bishop Museum on Oahu sell beautiful Hawaiian-made objects. Hawaiian artists sell their work in the courtyard at the Dole Plantation and you'll find original arts and crafts at many of the farmer's markets. There are a few shops making Hawaii-inspired jewellery – Maui Divers and Na Hoku both sell gold and silver work with gemstones and pearls. For quality Ni`ihau shell *leis*, expect to pay hundreds of dollars.

Bailey House Museum ⓐ 2375 Main St, #A, Wailuku

Bishop Museum ⓐ 1525 Bernice St, Honolulu

SECOND-HAND & ANTIQUES

Treasure hunters and antique sleuths might enjoy the second-hand stores of Honoka`a on the Big Island or Honolulu's Chinatown. Wailuku on Maui has an amazing selection of shops selling Chinese antiques.

CONVENIENCE STORES

ABC stores are everywhere. You'll be able to get just about anything you need at the ABC store. And for all things Hawaiian, you can't beat Hilo Hattie's. Hilo Hattie's runs shuttle buses to their stores from many of the resort areas on the islands. If it's a souvenir or somehow Hawaii-related, Hilo Hattie's is sure to have it.

LIFESTYLE

Children

Hawaii has so many outdoor activities and hands-on exploration options that there's no reason for children to get restless. Many resorts offer amenities just for kids – ask the concierge for details. Restaurants often have kids' menus, too. Most tour providers welcome well-behaved younger guests, but ask if there's a minimum age requirement when you book your adventure to avoid disappointment.

Here are just a few suggestions – check with the Activities and Attractions Association of Hawaii (☎ 800 398 9698) for more ideas.

Dolphin Quest at the Hilton Waikaloa

Introduce your children to friendly Big Island residents – in the water! Those as young as five years old can meet the dolphins, nose-to-bottle-nose at Kids Quest; children over ten years old can participate in The Encounter. Programmes vary in price from $150 to $235.
☎ 886 2875 ⓦ http://dolphinquest.org ❶ Booking required

Full moon rock pooling

See tidal creatures by the light of the moon! The Maui-based Pacific Whale Foundation runs full moon rock pool tours that introduce curious children – and their parents – to the nocturnal inhabitants of the coastal zone. Children aged six and over are welcome. Wear sturdy shoes and bring a torch. Contact the Pacific Whale Foundation for more information at ☎ 249 8811 ⓦ www.pacificwhale.org
❶ Reservations required

Happy Trails Hawai`i Horseback Rides

This family-friendly riding outfit on Oahu prides itself on being able to allow children as young as six years old to ride safely on a horse of their own. ☎ 638 RIDE (7433) ⓦ www.happytrailshawaii.com
❶ Reservations required

Maui Ocean Center

Little ones too small to snorkel or who haven't learned to swim yet should still get a chance to see Hawaii's amazing sea life. Ocean Center Maui is a lovely little aquarium that has beautiful tanks of tropical fish, a sea turtle viewing area, an enormous tank for watching rays and sharks, tide pools that encourage you to touch the creatures and lots of educational opportunities. The centre also has quite a good restaurant that serves sustainable seafood options. At Ma`alaea Harbor.

ⓐ Maui Ocean Center 192 Ma`alaea Rd, Wailuku ☎ 270 7000

Oahu Hawaiian Waters Adventure Park

Kids love waterslides, even kids that are a bit more grown-up. From adrenaline-rushing drops into the big pools to leisurely floats, there's something for everyone at the park. There's a cafeteria, showers, changing rooms, souvenir stands.... If you've had enough of the sand but still want to get wet, this is the ideal place to play – day or night.

ⓦ www.hawaiianwaters.com

Sea Life Park

This Oahu park gives visitors an unusual level of interactivity with dolphins, sea lions and stingrays in a safe, supervised environment. There's a surprising exhibit with endangered penguins, which are thriving here in this unlikely home for an Arctic species. Call ahead to reserve your interactive activity. ☎ 866 DOLPHIN (365 7446)
ⓦ www.sealifeparkhawaii.com

Sports & activities

If it's an outdoor activity, you'll probably find it on Hawaii – even skiing, on rare occasions! While watersports reign supreme, Hawaii is also great for land-based sportspeople: golfers, cyclists, horse riders and ramblers. The best place to find activities is through Activities and Attractions Association of Hawaii. Call ☎ 800 398 9698 to get started.

DIVING & SNORKELLING
Each island offers diving and snorkelling options, from day trips to diver certification programmes. Boats leave from Keauhou Bay on the Big Island, Lahaina Harbor on Maui, Waikiki on Oahu, and Port Allen on Kauai. Most tour operators provide snorkel gear, but diving gear and wetsuits cost extra. Molokini, Lana`i and Kealakekua Bay are popular destinations, with their clear waters and diverse sea life.

GOLF
Hawaii offers more than 100 courses to choose from, ranging from publicly maintained greens to the exclusive Challenge on Lana`i.

◼ *Hawaii equals surfing*

Many of the resorts are partnered with spectacular courses – convenient if not all of your travellers are golfers! Most airlines count your clubs as one of your checked items as long as they're not overweight.

HORSE RIDING

The Hawaiian cowboy has been an icon since the Spanish brought cattle farming to the islands. As a result, horse-riding opportunities are plentiful. Try the Parker Ranch on the Big Island, Kualoa Ranch on Oahu, or Haleakala on Maui. You'll need long trousers and sturdy shoes. Many companies can accommodate young children: ask about age restrictions.

OUTRIGGERS, KAYAKS & MORE

The trip to Fern Grotto on the Wailua River on Kauai is fun to make by kayak, and tours also go to Kaleakakua Bay on the Big Island. Rentals are widely available and guided tours are easy to find. Outrigger adventures are a little less common, but are an exciting way to experience the waters.

SURFING

This most Hawaiian of activities was first recorded by the explorer Captain Cook in 1779. Petroglyphs and ancient chants dating back to 1500 mention surfing too. Surfing schools are everywhere – on the beach at Waikiki, Oahu's North Shore, in Kihei on Maui, at Hanalei on Kauai... Pick a small class, an experienced instructor, and be prepared to fall over.

WALKING

Hawaii's varied ecosystems mean that walkers can explore terrain that's hot and dry, cold and windy, wet and tropical...and end their walks at waterfalls, pools, steaming sulphur vents, even in the snow on Hawaii's peaks. The National Parks and ecotourism providers lead guided hikes to sacred sites on private land in places like the Waipi`o Valley or Halawa. Independent walkers might enjoy the trail up the Na Pali Cliffs on Kauai or a walk through the bamboo forest near `Ohe`o Gulch on Maui. As with any outdoor adventure, wear sturdy shoes, carry water and be prepared. Mosquito repellent is useful.

LIFESTYLE

Festivals & events

With Hawaii's melting pot of cultures, it seems as if there's always something happening that's worth celebrating, be it cultural, historical or agricultural. And in Hawaii's forgiving climate, the festivities are almost always outdoors. It's impossible to list everything here – check the local papers or with the tourism office to get full details of what is going on during your visit.

JANUARY
Jan–Feb: Narcissus Festival (Oahu) – Chinese cultural festival
Hula Bowl (Maui) – American college football tournament
Ka Molokai Makahiki (Molokai) – Hawaiian cultural festival
Maui Pro Surf Meet (Maui)

FEBRUARY
Feb–Mar: Cherry Blossom Festival (Oahu) – Japanese cultural festival
Great Maui Whale Festival (Maui)
Hilo Mardi Gras (Big Island)
NFL Pro Bowl (Honolulu, Oahu) – post-season professional American football game

MARCH
17 Mar: St Patrick's Day Parade (Waikiki, Oahu)
26 Mar: Prince Kuhio Day (state holiday)
Windward Orchid Society Annual Spring Show (Oahu)

APRIL
Easter Sunrise Service (Punchbowl Crater, Oahu)
Merrie Monarch Festival (Hilo, Big Island) – very popular cultural festival and *hula* competition

MAY

1 May: *Lei* Day (state holiday) – *lei*-making demonstrations and contests
3rd Sat: Molokai Ka *Hula* Piko (Molokai) – *hula* dance festival
International Festival of Canoes (Maui)

JUNE

11 June: King Kamehameha Day (state holiday) – parades, performances and craft fairs
June–Aug: O-Bon Festival – Japanese Buddhist festival and dances
Kiho`alu Hawaiian Slack-Key Guitar Festival (Maui)

JULY

4 July: Makawao Rodeo (Maui), Parker Ranch Rodeo (Big Island)
Hawaii International Jazz Festival (Honolulu, Oahu)
Koloa Plantation Days (Kauai) – celebration of Hawaiian sugar-cane industry
Pu`uhonua o Honaunau Cultural Festival (Big Island) – Hawaiian historical festival and royal court re-creation
Quicksilver Cup Windsurfing Competition (Maui)

△ *Polynesian cultural events are very popular*

AUGUST
Hawaiian International Billfish Tournament (Big Island) – big-game fishing invitational

SEPTEMBER
Sept–Oct: *Aloha* Week – Hawaii's largest arts and cultural festival, held for one week on each island
A Taste of Lahaina (Maui) – culinary and tasting festival

OCTOBER
31 Oct: Halloween Parade (Lahaina, Maui & Waikiki, Oahu)
Oct–Nov: *Aloha* Classic Windsurfing Championships (Maui)
Hamakua Music Festival (Big Island)
Ironman Triathlon World Championship (Big Island)
Na Molokai Hoe (Molokai) – outrigger canoe race to Oahu

NOVEMBER
Nov–Dec: Triple Crown of Surfing World Cup (Oahu)
Hawaii International Film Festival (Oahu, other islands)
Kona Coffee Cultural Festival (Big Island)
Mission Houses Museum Holiday Crafts Fair (Honolulu, Oahu)
World Invitation *Hula* Festival (Honolulu, Oahu)

DECEMBER
2nd Sun: Honolulu Marathon (Oahu)
25 Dec: Hawaii Bowl (Honolulu, Oahu) – US college football tournament
Honolulu City Lights (Oahu) – Christmas-tree lighting festival
Na Mele O Maui (Ka`anapali, Maui) – Hawaiian cultural and music festival
PGA Grand Slam (Kauai) – championship golf tournament

▶ *Bronze hula statue at Kona International Airport*

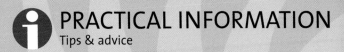

Accommodation

Rooms average about US$200 per night, but budget travellers can find private rooms for as low as US$60 a night. Price guidelines are as follows: £ under US$180   ££ US$180–300   £££ over US$300

OAHU
Diamond Head Beach Hotel £ Walking distance from the lights of Waikiki. Beach access. ⓐ 2947 Kalakaua Ave, Honolulu ☏ 922 1928

Waikiki Grand Hotel £ Conveniently located just off 'the strip' in Waikiki. ⓐ 134 Kapahulu Ave, Honolulu ☏ 923 1814 ⓦ www.waikikigrand.com

HAWAII
Kona Bay Hotel £ A popular central choice for backpackers and budget travellers. ⓐ 75-5739 Ali`i Drive, Kailua-Kona ☏ 329 1393

Uncle Billy's £ Hawaiian-run, affordable and conveniently located hotels in the centre of Kailua-Kona Village and in central Hilo. ⓦ www.unclebilly.com

Kona Village Resort £££ All-inclusive beachfront getaway. ⓐ Queen Ka`ahumanu Highway, Kailua-Kona ☏ 367 5290 ⓦ www.konavillage.com

KAUAI
Kauai International Hostel £ In lively Kapa`a town. Probably the cheapest beds on the island. ⓐ 4532 Lehua St, Kapa`a ☏ 823 6142 ⓦ www.kauaiinternationalhostel.com

Grand Hyatt Kauai Resort and Spa £££ Extensive beachfront resort complex with beach access, and an amazing network of swimming pools. ⓐ 1571 Poi`pu Rd ☏ 240 6436 ⓦ www.grandhyattkauai.com

MAUI

Lahaina Shores Resort £ Studio and one-bedroom apartments near the harbour. ⓐ 475 Front St, Lahaina ⓣ 381 3631
ⓦ http://lahainashores-px.rtrk.com

Maui Vista Resort £ Apartments with full kitchens, walking distance from Kihei Beaches. Good for families. ⓐ 2191 South Kihei Rd, Kihei
ⓣ 879 7966 ⓦ www.alohamauivista.com

MOLOKAI

Molokai Vacation Rental £–££ Apartment rentals in a handful of developed resorts throughout Molokai. Facilities vary. ⓣ 800 367 2984
ⓦ www.molokai-vacation-rental.com

Hotel Molokai ££ Polynesian-style rooms with kitchen facilities. Close to town. ⓐ Kamehameha V Highway, Kaunakakai, Molokai
ⓣ 800 535 0085 ⓦ www.hotelmolokai.com

LANA`I

**Hotel Lana`i ££** Attractive little hotel in Lana`i City. The restaurant specialises in Hawaii Regional Cuisine and attracts lots of locals.
ⓐ 828 Lana`i Ave, Lana`i City ⓣ 565 7211 ⓦ www.hotellanai.com

The Lodge at Keole £££ Luxury resort above Lana`i City, on the golf course. ⓐ One Keomoku Highway, Lana`i City ⓣ 565 4000
ⓦ www.fourseasons.com/koele

ALL ISLANDS

Bed and Breakfast Hawaii £–£££ Books B&Bs on all of the islands.
ⓣ 733 1632 ⓦ www.bandb-hawaii.com

Castle Resorts and Hotels ££–£££ Offer 3- to 5-star hotels and condos on all five main islands. ⓣ 545 3510 ⓦ www.castleresorts.com

Preparing to go

GETTING THERE
Flying

The quickest and least expensive route to Hawaii from the UK is flying via the West Coast of the USA or Canada. It's possible to get non-stop flights to Hawaii from Los Angeles, San Francisco and Seattle in the USA and Vancouver in Canada. The trip takes approximately five hours from the West Coast. You may find it most convenient to book your long-haul flight from Britain on one carrier and use a West Coast carrier for transportation to Hawaii.

Northwest, KLM and British Airways offer non-stop flights from the UK to the West Coast. United, American, Alaska and Hawaiian airlines all offer flights from the West Coast to Hawaii. Air Canada flies direct from Vancouver. Non-stop flights from the UK to the West Coast take between nine and ten hours; itineraries via the East Coast can take considerably longer.

Alaska Airlines ❶ 2527 5200 ⓦ www.alaskaair.com
American Airlines ❶ 20 7365 0777 ⓦ www.americanairlines.co.uk
British Airways ❶ 0870 850 9 850 ⓦ www.britishairways.com
Hawaiian Airlines ❶ 1 367 5320 ⓦ www.hawaiianair.com
Northwest Airlines/KLM ❶ 08705 074074
ⓦ www.nwa.com/www.klm.com
United Airlines ❶ 0845 8 444 777 ⓦ www.unitedairlines.co.uk

Many people are aware that air travel emits CO_2, which contributes to climate change. You may be interested in the possibility of lessening the environmental impact of your flight through the charity Climate Care, which offsets your CO_2 by funding environmental projects around the world. Visit ⓦ www.climatecare.org

Cruises from the mainland

There are a few cruise lines that cross the Pacific from the West Coast. Princess Cruises offers a sailing from Los Angeles. Holland-America departs from Seattle, Washington, San Diego, California, or Vancouver,

British Columbia. The crossing takes between 4 and 6 days, depending on your port of departure.

Holland America Line UK ☎ 0845 351 0557 Ⓦ www.hollandamerica.com
Norwegian Cruise Line ☎ 00800 0310 21 21 Ⓦ www.ncl.eu
Princess Cruises ☎ 0845 075 0031 Ⓦ www.princess.com

Package options

Many airline carriers offer good-value holiday package deals that include the airfare, accommodation and car rental. Cruise packages may include excursions and overnight stays in island hotels – ask your booking agent about what's available.

TOURIST INFORMATION

The Hawaii Tourism office operates a website that's full of useful information for planning your trip. The Hawaii-based Visitors and Convention Bureau operates a more comprehensive site.

Go Hawaii, Hawaii Visitors and Convention Bureau ☎ 1 800 GOHAWAII (464 29244) Ⓦ www.gohawaii.com
Hawaii Tourism Europe ☎ 020 7367 0900
Ⓦ www.hawaii-tourism.co.uk

BEFORE YOU LEAVE

Travellers should have no trouble purchasing anything they need while in Hawaii, but it's always a good idea to bring copies of any prescription medicines you might need. No inoculations are needed.

You may want to consider purchasing travel and medical insurance simply because of the high cost of extensive medical treatment in Hawaii. Check policies carefully for coverage of medical expenses, loss of baggage or travel documents. If you are going to indulge in sports such as scuba diving, ensure these are covered by your insurance policy.

ENTRY FORMALITIES

Hawaii has the same entry conditions as the rest of the USA: citizens of the UK, Ireland, Canada, Australia and New Zealand need a valid

○ *Cruise liners travel from the States*

passport, must stay fewer than 90 days, have a return or onward ticket and enter on an airline or cruise ship in the visa waiver programme (which includes all major carriers). US citizens need official ID in order to board a plane, such as a driver's licence. Citizens of South Africa must get a visa from their local US embassy or consulate (ⓦ www.pretoria.usembassy.gov).

If you're stopping on the US mainland before you transfer to Hawaii, be aware that you will need to clear customs. Allow yourself plenty of transit time when booking your trip. If you are going through Canada, you will clear US customs upon arrival in Hawaii. If you're transferring to an inter-island flight on arrival, again, be sure to allow yourself enough time to clear US customs.

MONEY

The US dollar (US$) comes in notes of $1, $5, $10, $20, $50 and $100. Notes are all the same size and colour. One dollar equals 100 cents (¢), with coins of 1 cent (penny), 5 cents (nickel), 10 cents (dime) and 25 cents (quarter). Quarters are handy for laundry and public transport.

ATMs are plentiful and can often be found in supermarkets and convenience stores. Credit cards are widely accepted. Check with your bank about exchange fees on credit card and ATM purchases. ATMs and credit cards are easier and more convenient choices than currency exchange offices, which are not that common.

CLIMATE

Hawaii has a broad variety of microclimates – you can go from the summit of Mauna Loa to a hot sandy beach in the same day. The evenings can be cool and windy. In wetter areas like Hilo or Hana, rain is not unusual.

Mild weather is the norm in the islands, with the winter season, October to April, having slightly cloudier or rainy days. June to November is considered hurricane season, but hurricanes are very rare. Water temperatures average a very pleasant 22°C (72°F). The biggest weather-related risk for travellers is likely to be sunburn.

There is really no bad time to visit Hawaii, though the trade winds can affect surf and sailing conditions and limit the visibility in the water for snorkellers and divers.

BAGGAGE ALLOWANCE

Baggage allowances vary according to the airline, destination and class of travel, and also – at the moment – to which airport you are leaving from. US carriers may also have different baggage restrictions from international carriers. It's always best to get updated baggage allowances from your airline prior to your departure.

Complicated restrictions imposed in the USA can make it confusing to know exactly what is allowable in your checked or carry-on luggage. If you're not sure, err on the conservative side and don't pack it. Check the Transportation Security Administration website prior to your departure for the latest news on baggage restrictions.

Transportation Security Administration Ⓦ www.tsa.gov

Note that if you're using public transport instead of the privately operated airport shuttles, you are only allowed one bag.

During your stay

AIRPORTS

There are three international airports, in Kona and Hilo on the Big Island and in Honolulu on Oahu. The other islands operate smaller facilities that serve the inter-island flights.

The **Airport Waikiki Express** runs passengers from Oahu's airport to any hotel in Waikiki, leaving every 20–25 minutes for $9 or $15 return (☎ 866 898 2519 🌐 www.robertshawaii.com).

On Maui and the Big Island, the **SpeediShuttle** serves Kahului and Kona airports respectively; call or see the website for fares and reservations. ☎ 877 242 5777 🌐 www.speedishuttle.com

TheBus, Oahu's public transport system, operates two lines to and from Honolulu airport, but since large luggage items are not allowed on board (all bags must fit under a seat or on your lap), most visitors are likely to need to use a taxi or hire car instead. The fare on TheBus is $2.

Taxis can be hailed on the street in Honolulu and Waikiki; everywhere else they must be ordered by phone. Although fares are metered, be sure to ask about approximate prices before you get in. From Waikiki to Honolulu International Airport, expect to pay around $30–40. Tips of 10–15 per cent are customary.

COMMUNICATIONS
Telephoning

Hawaii's area code is 808, and the country code for the USA is 1. To dial local (i.e. same island) calls, just dial the 7-digit number; to call inter-island dial 1 808 and then the number. For other US states, dial 1, then the area code and number. Toll-free (freephone) numbers start with 800, 888, 866 or 877, and can be made free of charge from public phones. Beware of higher prices when calling from hotel rooms.

Public telephones cost 50 cents for a local call. Pre-paid phone cards for local or international calls can be bought at newsagents and convenience stores. Directory enquiries can be reached on 411 for local listings or ☎ 1 808 555 1212 for listings on other islands.

To use an international mobile phone in Hawaii with a local SIM chip, you'll need a multi-band phone that will work on 850 and 1900 MHz.

TELEPHONING ABROAD

To place an international call, first dial 011, then the country code, and then the number. Area codes may need to be preceded by a zero; this varies according to the country you're dialling.

The country code for the United Kingdom is 44, Ireland 353, South Africa 27, Australia 61 and New Zealand 64. For other country codes, check the front of the phone book, or dial the operator (411) and ask for assistance in placing your call.

Postal service

All towns in the islands have a US postal service office or agent, usually open from 08.30 to 16.00 on weekdays and for a few hours (variable) on Saturday mornings. Some hotels and gift shops also sell stamps. Postboxes are blue. Sending international postcards costs 90¢; letters are by weight and also start at 90¢.

Internet access

Many hotels, restaurants and cafés offer free wi-fi internet to those with their own laptops. Larger hotels usually have internet terminals for guests – sometimes for free, sometimes for an hourly charge. Internet cafés are available but not common, and prices are usually not very cheap. Some youth hostels offer their internet terminals to non-guests at lower prices. Public libraries have free internet terminals for patrons; visitors can obtain a three-month library card for $10.

CUSTOMS

Casual dress is the standard for most places; even in the more upmarket restaurants, shorts and bare shoulders are widely accepted, though some of the finer restaurants and clubs have a dress code. Nude or topless sunbathing is not widely permitted.

ELECTRICITY

Like all US states, Hawaii uses 110–120 volts and the standard US plug with two flat parallel prongs. 220-volt appliances will need a converter and a plug adaptor.

EMERGENCIES

Hawaii has Western-quality health care and facilities, and clinics or hospitals with emergency (casualty) wards can be found just about everywhere. As you might expect, the smaller islands have less extensive facilities, while the best hospitals are in Honolulu. Your hotel can help you find a local doctor or dentist, or consult the local directory. Consultation fees usually start around US$100 and, even if you have insurance, you'll need to pay up front and claim the costs back later. All hospitals and most doctors' surgeries will take credit cards, although smaller doctors' surgeries may prefer cash. Ensure you keep all your medical receipts for claim purposes.

Coast Guard Emergency 1 808 842 2600
Emergencies (Police, Ambulance, Fire) 911

Embassies & consulates

All foreign embassies are in Washington, DC. Only Australia has a consulate in Hawaii.

Australia 1000 Bishop Street, Penthouse Suite, Honolulu, HI 96813
524 5050
1601 Massachusetts Ave NW, Washington, DC 20036 202 797 3000
www.austemb.org
Canada 501 Pennsylvania Ave NW, Washington, DC 20001 202 682 1740 www.canadianembassy.org
New Zealand 37 Observatory Circle NW, Washington, DC 20008
202 328 4800 www.nzemb.org
South Africa 3051 Massachusetts Ave NW, Washington, DC 20008
202 232 4400 www.saembassy.org
United Kingdom 3100 Massachusetts Ave NW, Washington, DC 20008
202 588 6640 www.britainusa.com

GETTING AROUND

Although the islands are not large, sights are spread out and most visitors hire a car; otherwise you may have to rely on hotel guest shuttles. Travel to other islands is via short plane trips.

Bicycles, motorcycles & scooters

Bikes are available for hire in all tourist areas, generally for use around town (not for long-distance touring). Another option is 'downhill cycling', where you and your bike are driven somewhere high up so you can ride back down without pedalling (Maui's Haleakala Crater is a popular option). Motorcycles and scooters can also be hired; helmets are required for riders aged under 18.

Buses

Oahu, the most populated island, has an excellent public transport system that's fully sufficient for travel around Waikiki and Honolulu. It does cover the rest of the island, but if you'd like to go exploring you'll find a hire car will let you get around faster and on your own schedule. The other islands have no reliable transport system beyond a few hotel or local shuttles, so unless you plan to stay in one small town or resort, you'll almost certainly want to hire a car.

The routes of Oahu's excellent TheBus system cover the entire island. See the website for maps and timetables, or ask your hotel for a system map. Fares are paid in cash (have the exact amount ready in notes or silver coins – drivers cannot give change) or by pre-paid pass: at the time of writing, fares were $2 for adults, $1 for children aged 6–17 years, and free for children under 6 (when accompanied by a paying adult). Ask for a free transfer when you board – you can use it for another ride within two hours. All buses are accessible to those with disabilities. TheBus also has two lines to and from the airport, but since large luggage items are not allowed on board (all bags must fit under a seat or on your lap), most visitors will need to use a taxi or hire car.

All stops are indicated with a yellow 'TheBus' sign.

TheBus ☎ 848 5555 Ⓦ www.thebus.org

Cars

Hired cars, vans and jeeps are the most popular way to get around the island: major companies include Alamo, Avis, Budget, Dollar, Hertz and National. Molokai has Budget and Dollar, while Lana`i has only Lana`i City Service (☎ 565 7227).

Drivers must be over 21 (or sometimes 25) and have a valid driving licence and a credit card. It's a good idea to book in advance; rates begin around $35 per day and some companies offer weekly discounts. Unless your credit card or trip insurance covers it, you may want to opt for the Loss Damage Waiver (LDW), as under Hawaii law you will be responsible for any damage regardless of fault. Gas (petrol) stations can be far apart in remoter areas, so fill up when you can and monitor levels carefully.

Roads in Hawaii are generally up to Western standards, although some minor roads in rural areas may be unpaved or in inferior condition. Enquire with your car hire company about their unpaved road regulations. The speed limit on interstate highways is 55 mph (90 km/h), but otherwise are generally 25–35 mph (40–55 km/h); many narrow, winding coastal roads (such as Maui's Hana Highway or Molokai's east coast) can go down to 5–10 mph (8–16 km/h).

Seat belts are mandatory for everyone in the car, and pedestrians always have right of way. Right turns at red lights are permitted after coming to a complete stop, unless there is a sign to the contrary. Traffic in Hawaii, as in all US states, drives on the right.

Taxis

Taxis can be hailed on the street in Honolulu and Waikiki; everywhere else they must be booked by telephone. Although fares are metered, make sure you ask about approximate prices up front. Tips of 10–15 per cent are customary.

Inter-island transportation
Aeroplane

With the islands so close together, planes are the main method for inter-island transport for visitors and locals alike – most flights are only

30–45 minutes long, although some routes require connecting flights through Honolulu. Five carriers and dozens of flights daily make for competitive pricing, so check websites for the best deals. Aloha and Hawaiian have the most flights and largest planes, and service all the islands as well as some US mainland and international destinations. Island, Pacific Wings/PW Express and go! feature mid-size and smaller planes and may be a better bet for flights to Molokai or Lana`i.

go! ☎ 888 IFLYGO 2 ⓦ www.iflygo.com
Hawaiian ☎ 800 882 8811 ⓦ www.hawaiianair.com
Island ☎ 484 2222 ⓦ www.islandair.com
Pacific Wings ☎ 888 575 4546 ⓦ www.pacificwings.com

Ferry
The giant SuperFerry sails passengers and cars from Oahu to Maui and Kauai (three hours), with a route to the Big Island (four and a half hours) scheduled for 2009. Two smaller ships also sail from Lahaina on Maui to Molokai (90 minutes) or Lana`i (45 minutes).
Lana`i Ferry ☎ 800 695 2624 ⓦ www.go-lanai.com
Molokai Ferry ☎ 866 307 6524 ⓦ www.molokaiferry.com
SuperFerry ☎ 877 HI FERRY ⓦ www.hawaiisuperferry.com

HEALTH, SAFETY & CRIME
Hawaii has little in the way of health hazards. Mosquitoes are a nuisance, but they don't carry malaria. Insect repellent can be found at supermarkets, convenience stores and pharmacies. Walkers should keep an eye out for scorpions and spiders.

Ocean safety is extremely important. The currents are very strong, especially in winter, and every year a few dozen visitors drown off Hawaii's shores. Always swim between the flags and in sight of lifeguards; if a beach is not guarded, assess water conditions carefully, stay close to shore and don't swim alone. Never turn your back on the ocean – sudden rogue waves can sweep you out to sea. Heed signs regarding dangerous rocks or coral, rips or currents and shore breaks.

If you get carried out by a current, stay calm and don't swim against it (you'll tire yourself out) – wait until it dissipates, usually around 90 m (300 ft) from the shore, then swim to either side, out of the current, and back to shore. If you cut yourself on coral, ensure you clean the wound thoroughly with antiseptic.

Sunburn and dehydration are always a danger in the tropics. Be sure to wear high SPF sunscreen and protective clothing, and drink plenty of water. The sun is strongest from 11.00 to 14.00, so consider staying under cover or indoors at these times for the first few days. If you plan to snorkel, wear a t-shirt to protect your back and shoulders.

Violent crime is rare in Hawaii, but, as with any tourist area, theft can be a problem. Never leave any valuables in a parked car when you're off sightseeing or at the beach. Use common sense when walking alone at night, especially in remote areas. Use hotel safes to store passports, extra cash, jewellery and expensive electronics.

MEDIA
Newspapers & magazines
Hawaii has two state-wide newspapers, the *Honolulu Advertiser* and the *Honolulu Star-Bulletin*, and Hawai`i Island, Maui and Kauai all have daily and weekly papers, while Molokai has two weekly papers. National and international papers can be found in Honolulu, Waikiki and major hotels or tourist areas on the other islands.

Broadcast media
Most hotel rooms have cable or satellite TVs that receive all the US channels. Local and state radio stations generally feature classical and pop music, news and talk radio and Christian programming.

OPENING HOURS
Banks ◷ 08.30–15.30 Mon–Thur, 08.30–18.00 Fri, and sometimes Saturday mornings.
Businesses (airline offices, etc.) ◷ 09.00–17.00 Mon–Fri.
Shops Trading hours vary, but most shops are open from around 10.00

to around 17.00, except in Waikiki, tourist areas and large shopping centres, where they may stay open as late as 22.00 (earlier on Sundays). Most stores are also open on Sundays, and some supermarkets and many convenience stores are open 24 hours a day, seven days a week.

RELIGION

Missionaries brought Christianity to the islands, suppressing the native Hawaiian culture, but the ancient gods and goddesses live on in the practices of *hula* and storytelling. Christianity is dominant, but Buddhism, Judaism, Islam and Hinduism are also practised.

TAXES

Hawaii's sales tax on goods and services is 4.17 per cent; on hotel rooms it's 11.42 per cent. Keep in mind that most prices are quoted before tax, so your total will always be a bit higher than the original price. Some hotels levy additional fees during high season, so be sure to ask when booking.

TIME DIFFERENCES

Hawaii has its own time zone – Hawaiian Standard Time (HST) – but unlike mainland USA does not observe Daylight Savings Time in summer; the time difference thus increases by 1 hour for other countries that use DST. On standard time, Hawaii is 2 hours behind the US West Coast, 5 hours behind the US East Coast, 10 hours behind the UK, 12 hours behind South Africa, 20 hours behind the Australian East Coast and 22 hours behind New Zealand.

TIPPING

Tipping is customary in Hawaii for service jobs: 15 per cent is the standard minimum in restaurants (unless service is included in the bill), 10 to 15 per cent for taxi drivers, $1 per drink in bars, $1 per piece of luggage for bellboys, $1 per night for housekeeping staff and $1–2 for

valet parking attendants. (More is always appreciated if you wish to reward particularly good service.)

TOILETS

Free public toilets of normal Western standards are available in nearly all shopping centres, hotels and state parks. Many restaurants will also allow non-patrons to use their toilets on request (although some smaller places may reserve them only for customers). Some toilets are labelled in Hawaiian: *kane* (men) and *wahine* (women). Many beaches have only portable toilets for use; it's a good idea to have some toilet paper or tissues on hand for these.

TRAVELLERS WITH DISABILITIES

Hawaii is very welcoming to those with disabilities. Hotels, restaurants, buses and state parks have reserved parking, ramps and accessible toilets, and Avis and Hertz offer hire cars with hand controls if booked well in advance.

The Disability and Communication Access Board offers information on accessible destinations, interpreters and other support services around the islands, and the Society for Accessible Travel and Hospitality can also offer advice and information.

Disability and Communication Access Board 📞 586 8121
🌐 www.hawaii.gov/health/dcab/travel
Society for Accessible Travel and Hospitality 🌐 www.sath.org

ACKNOWLEDGEMENTS

We would like to thank all the photographers, picture libraries and organisations for the loan of the photographs reproduced in this book, to whom copyright in the photograph belongs:

David Olsen/Getty Images (pages 10–11); Alvis Upitis/Getty Images (page 35); Ann Cecil/Getty Images (page 37); Peter French/Jason Fujii/Getty Images (page 47); World Pictures/Photoshot (pages 1, 5, 13, 31, 43, 50, 59, 62, 66, 72, 95, 107); all the rest, Pam Mandel.

Project editor: Penny Isaac
Layout: Donna Pedley
Proofreader: Karolin Thomas
Indexer: Karolin Thomas

Send your thoughts to
books@thomascook.com

- Found a beach bar, peaceful stretch of sand or must-see sight that we don't feature?

- Like to tip us off about any information that needs a little updating?

- Want to tell us what you love about this handy little guidebook and, more importantly, how we can make it even handier?

Then here's your chance to tell all! Send us ideas, discoveries and recommendations today and then look out for your valuable input in the next edition of this title.

Email to the above address or write to:
HotSpots Series Editor, Thomas Cook Publishing, PO Box 227, Unit 9, Coningsby Road, Peterborough PE3 8SB, UK.